STANDPIPE

DELIVERING WATER
IN FLINT

STANDPIPE

DELIVERING WATER
IN FLINT

DAVID HARDIN

Belt Publishing

Printed in the United States of America
First edition 2021
1 2 3 4 5 6 7 8 9

ISBN: 978-1-948742-82-5

Belt Publishing
5322 Fleet Avenue
Cleveland, Ohio 44105
www.beltpublishing.com

Cover by David Wilson
Book design by Meredith Pangrace

For Sue. So, it shall always be.

"He'd grown up on endlessness and his mother.
In the beginning, they were the same thing."

—Philip Roth, *Sabbath's Theater*

Have a blessed day, I'm told over and over again. I've never felt so blessed. Kindness, bestowed by people too bereft of surplus to warrant such generosity. I'm grateful, but my gratitude is leavened with a liberal dash of liberal guilt. I wince despite myself every time I hear it uttered. Repetition dulls the sting. Liberated by banality, I mourn the loss.

ONE

Late February, 2016, I complete training and qualify as a Red Cross Disaster Relief Volunteer (DRV) behind the wheel of a boxy, red and white Red Cross Emergency Response Vehicle (ERV). I deploy to an officially declared Disaster Relief Operation in Flint, Michigan—city long on the wane, lately devastated by a municipal water supply contaminated with dangerous levels of lead. Children and the aged are at greatest risk. A local pediatrician is among the first citizens to sound the alarm, spurred to action by a rash of symptoms turning up in her young patients. By early 2016, the men, women, and children of Flint have been drinking lead-contaminated water, far in excess of federal safety standards, for many months. Widespread lead contamination is, sadly, become common place. But in 2016, Flint is novel among that unfortunate club of communities devastated by man-made disasters sexy enough to have captured the public's fickle imagination. Right up there with Three Mile Island (Pennsylvania), the Upper Big Branch Mine Disaster (West Virginia), Love Canal (New York), and Times Beach (Missouri).

The seeds of the crisis had been planted over a year before, in 2014. I deploy to a city for which I have no particular affinity, nor harbor any bad blood. Just another town through which I've passed free of claim, like Camden, Maine; Greenville, South Carolina; or Great Falls, Montana. Unlike those other places, however, Flint is only a ninety-minute drive north from where I live, home to fellow Michiganders—trolls like me, living *below* the Mackinac Bridge. My taxes went to pay the salaries of the men responsible for the disaster and those endeavoring to deflect responsibility and avoid criminal prosecution. Michigan taxpayers and the citizens of Flint will foot much of the bill and endure all of the heartache for a scheme borne of market solution, anti-tax, small government machinations. What happened in Flint could happen to any community. It could happen to mine, but that's unlikely. I live in a mostly white, financially solvent suburb just north of Detroit. The majority Black citizens of Flint were considered politically irrelevant and socially expendable by those in power long before their water supply was contaminated with lead. Flint, like other poor communities of color around the state, is much more likely to suffer the disastrous consequences of ideological social engineering put to practice.

My mother, Ima Nell Hardin, began showing the first signs of decline that will lead to her eventual death, around the time Flint's water troubles began. We were inseparable my first five years, moon and planet in symbiotic orbit around my often absent yet omnipresent father.

Gene Hardin had escaped north from impoverished east Tennessee a few years after returning from the war. He fled a dirt-poor tobacco patch in the shadow of Great Smoky Mountain National Park. Freed himself from a tyrannical grandfather, a cold, overbearing mother, and a father bullied into submissive silence. He never looked back on the twilight hollow of his unhappy childhood. He was lured to Michigan by good paying union work in the lower tier of the automobile industry—hauling new Chryslers to small towns throughout Ohio, Pennsylvania, and West Virginia. Ima Nell married him straight out of high school, where she had demurred on academics for an independent study in the gossamer web of dewy boy-and-girl romance, patiently waiting for eligible prey to light, unawares. Together, they fled south across the Georgia state line to marry in a hasty civil ceremony, before lighting off for the territories—Hamtramck, Michigan.

Hamtramck, then as now, is a point of entry for immigrants from around the world, hungry for work, opportunity, and a better life for their children. When my Southern parents arrived, they washed ashore well behind established beachheads of Great Migration African Americans, Poles, and other eastern and southern Europeans, refugees displaced by war, pogrom, revolution, and Jim Crow. Many had prospered sufficiently to purchase homes elsewhere. Poles and Italians north along Gratiot Avenue, then out beyond Eight Mile Road. Jews and Chaldeans to points north and west. Latinos to the southwest side, and north to the orchard land of Macomb County. White southerners, south and southwest to cities like Lincoln Park, Taylor, and Romulus. African Americans had thrived since the nineteenth century in vibrant Black Bottom, just east of downtown Detroit, but were red-lined to isolated enclaves scattered throughout the metropolitan area after that neighborhood was razed to make way for a major freeway. Gene and Ima Nell followed Gratiot north, settling two miles beyond the Detroit city limits.

Ima Nell adjusted to the isolation of the new suburb, the long, lonely nights, family 600 miles distant. They may as well have been an ocean away in the Old Country. Her constant companion was the radio until I came along. Between that first Hamtramck apartment and our small brick ranch on a tract carved from old orchard, they had rented a flat on East Grand Boulevard near Belle Isle. Only a few years earlier, in the early years of the war, the island park was the scene of a bloody race riot between newly arrived Southern whites and vested Black auto workers. She worked for a time in the office of a downtown Detroit life insurance company, putting her typing skills to use. She loved the work; loved the freedom and the thrill of sidewalks teeming with postwar optimism.

Gene was on the road much of the time during their first decade in Michigan, returning home to shower, sleep, and eat before heading out once again. He didn't share her enthusiasm for the maddening crowd, her yearning for home. I wonder whether it had ever been his intention to anchor himself to one particular place, the intense desire to escape his guiding light. With a mortgage hanging over his head, a second child on the scene, roots firmly planted in northern soil, Gene's discontent flowered and spread like kudzu. I was drawn to him like a moth to a flame, but my desire for my father made it necessary to renounce my mother and deny the strong bond we had once enjoyed—I learned to marginalize her in order to curry his favor. Likewise, she was obliged to choose.

If I had to explain in two words our shared dilemma, I would be tempted to offer up the obscure nugget, *Hobson's Choice*. I don't mean to suggest that Thomas Hobson, English liveryman who lent his name to the dilemma of being forced to choose between two objectionable options or nothing at all, is implicated in my decision to volunteer with the Red Cross in Flint. Had I not gone, life would have continued on its familiar arc. Flint wouldn't have missed me in the slightest. At the same time, my long estrangement from my mother, ending with her death, had everything to do with my going to Flint. Flint transformed me. Or, rather, it was the first step in a long journey of transformation.

She was self-centered, manipulative, and could be childish and petulant when it suited her, but she loved me with singular ferocity, and I, her. We grew apart—gingerly, civilly, but not without mutual wounds of recrimination.

Nearly midway through the second decade of the new century, with her condition deteriorating, independence evaporating, I find myself longing for reconciliation, but wary of entanglement, fearful of succumbing to her overwhelming need. Fearful, too, of facing the truth. I need her badly. Maybe far more than she needs me.

Flint. A river runs through it, though more industrial trough than robust waterway. The river and city are on the cusp of worldwide notoriety. In less than two years, grieving my mother's death, I will find myself prowling the city's streets in my official capacity as disaster volunteer. But today, I'm mired in worries of my own.

TWO

Flint is boxed in north and south, east and west, by interstate highway and a bypass, a web of concrete and asphalt built chiefly to serve the needs of industry. On maps, the city is situated on the mound of a sprawling, industrial-sized baseball diamond—the chemical plants and refineries of Sarnia, Ontario at first base; Saginaw's automotive suppliers and Midland's Dow Chemical on second; Lansing's auto plants and the state capital holding down third; Detroit calling pitches behind home plate. Balance a bat along an axis between Grand Rapids and London, Ontario—Flint is your fulcrum.

Beyond the baseline, table-flat farmland extends north into Michigan's thumb, endless outfield where they raise sugar beets, soy beans, corn, and a particular strain of anti-government libertarianism. The McVeigh brothers, Timothy and James, along with accomplice Terry Nichols, once called Michigan's thumb home. Budding domestic terrorists, they perfected homemade fertilizer bombs in the endless, isolated, corduroy expanse of plowed fields and distant wind breaks. Hit a long fly ball and, if the wind is right, watch it carry left past West Branch for an out-of-the-park home run, ricocheting among white pine and jack pine forests up north. Unless, of course, it drifts foul into shallow Saginaw Bay.

THREE

I deploy to Flint, wary of the city's *Action News* reputation for mayhem, alert to the very real human cost of grinding, generational poverty. My heart is with the city's residents. My natural inclination, to side with the underdog. Most, but not all, of the people who will invite me into their homes over the coming months are people of color. All, with few exceptions, are poor. My colleagues in the water delivery business are, for the most part, white, from somewhere outside the city. Circumstances have conspired to bring us all together in wholly unpredictable ways. If *I'm* feeling anxious, uncertain as to whom and what I'll encounter, imagine the people peering out from behind all those front doors. For all my ambivalence about my reasons for being here—swooping in to save the thirsty people of Flint, or simply lending a hand to neighbors in need—imagine life on the receiving end. Decades of insult on top of injury, a people asked to pay the price, once again, for this nation's original sin. I'd grown up confused, listening to my father's casual racism, bias born of resentment. I recall as a small child visiting Tennessee with my family, sitting with him and my maternal grandfather on the screen porch, asking whether there were any "colored people" living there. I'd never seen anyone of color on our trips south. They erupted in gales of laughter. My face burned, the joke on me, neither of them seeing fit to explain the punchline. I'd grown up with every advantage, rejected my father's bitterness, but was slow to appreciate just how lucky I was. Now, newly arrived in Flint, stoked with righteous rage, I'm keenly aware of just how charmed a life I've led. Over the coming months, I'll meet hundreds of

Flint residents. We'll endure many awkward encounters and enjoy occasional moments of grace.

I begin my first day in the flatly fluorescent bowels of the Genesee County Sheriff's Department Emergency Command Center in downtown Flint. Uniformed officers, State Police troopers, and Michigan National Guardsman sit around a table in a too-warm, windowless basement. They chat, drink coffee, and manage to look casually lethal, drowsily blasé, and vigilant as Dobermans, all at the same time. We've come to retrieve a tactical radio transmitter that will, when activated, summon armed officers faster than a frantic call through the 911 system. At least that's what I'm told. I feel as though we're about to leave the safety of some blast-walled Green Zone, heedless of the caution implied by these taciturn veterans. The radio will serve as an unwelcome reminder on this, my first day, and all the days to come, of the messiness of delivering water in Flint. Our business concluded, short and sweet, we head back through the labyrinth of tiled corridors and echoing stairways and make our way outside. The sun is just coming up behind clouds of steel wool loaded with abraded shipyard gray.

Our first stop, a warehouse on the north side where tractor trailers unload pallets of bottled water from all over the lower forty-eight and Canada. We are handed the keys to a Penske box truck, wait in line to back up a loading ramp into a cavernous bay where we will receive the first two of the day's four pallets. Twenty burly men in camo Carhartt bibs and Cabela caps sit around a long table, chasing cigarettes with coffee, Red Bull, and Mountain Dew. Their role in the water game isn't readily apparent to me. Warehousing a single commodity in such vast quantities at such a rapid rate of turnover doesn't appear to require a great deal of manpower. Palleted H2O comes in one set of bays and goes out another. Two or three hi-lows move briskly, to and fro. My partner seems to know everyone, trades what passes for *bon mots* on a frigid mid-Michigan morning. Backing in takes three or four attempts before I clear the heavy steel door frame with less than an inch to spare. Everyone at the table is immersed, all-thumbs, in their bluish screens when I step down from the rig, studiously avoiding eye contact. No one pays me any mind.

I set about learning the nuts and bolts of the job, hustling cases of water from the high deck of the Penske truck into the houses, mobile homes, and apartments of the poor and infirm. It's not the first truck I've driven. Stake trucks, U-Hauls, hi-lows—once, during a summer stint on a landscaping crew, I was entrusted with a standard dump truck towing a trailer carrying a Ford tractor and bush hog mowing deck. Padding my scant truck driving experience is almost, but not quite, as subversively thrilling as sitting high up in a guttering cab, looking down into the private spaces of the lessor vehicular world.

Gene drove a truck for nearly fifty years. I remember looking out on Oakland Avenue in Highland Park, through the huge expanse of windshield from atop a teetering pile of canvas tarps, rain ponchos, and old log books onto the roofs of De Sotos, Valiants, and Coupe DeVilles. The cab was equipped with only one seat. The deafening roar of the engine, the dizzying height of my perch, and the acrid smell of diesel combined to terrify me, wanting only for the safety of my mother's arms. Greasy metallic fifth-wheel taste bitter in my mouth, I can still feel disappointment radiating off my father's massive shoulders like heat from a stack pipe.

The DRV's I meet are unfailingly nice. Many are retirees, proud veterans of Katrina or Sandy or flooding across the Mid-Atlantic, Upper Midwest, and Ozarks. They sport signature Red Cross wear: T-shirts, vests, and billed caps festooned with colorful service pins. I deploy in fits and starts. A snowy, late winter Friday; a sleet-driven Tuesday; a cold, drenched

Saturday followed by a brilliant Wednesday and a warm, damp Thursday. Eventually I will volunteer in Flint, Wednesdays mostly, February through July—a mere five months. Most DRVs in Flint deploy full time, as do a rotating group of young AmeriCorps volunteers. They live dormitory-style on stipend meals, drink bottled water, and take two-minute showers to minimize exposure to water-borne toxins. Six days a week, week after week, for months at a time. Some were here at the beginning, when water distribution was a slapdash affair, manning a logistical Wild West network of emergency distribution sites, the heavy presence of law enforcement and the military tinting the whole affair a flat, third-world shade of camo. My disaster relief vest helps dispel the nagging guilt of a slumming dilettante, but only a little.

FIVE

A case of twenty-four sixteen-ounce bottles of water weighs about thirty pounds. Stacking reduces the footprint, but concentrates structural load in one small area. It exerts pressure on the bottles in the bottommost cases, increasing the risk of leakage and water damage to subfloor and joists. Distribute your water—don't stack the cases too high, I advise people living in tiny bungalows, claustrophobic flats, cramped apartments, and ramshackle mobile homes. Living room floor space is given to entertainment centers, oxygen machines, cluttered coffee tables, sway-backed sofas, cockeyed recliners, space heaters, wheelchairs, walkers, toys, game systems, bird cages, Richard Serra-scale flat-screen televisions, pet beds, playpens, hospital beds, bureaus, book cases, animal crates, grandfather clocks, curio cabinets, murky aquariums, and dinette sets.

Kitchen counter space goes to coffee makers, blenders, toasters, pots and pans, liquor and wine bottles, plastic food storage containers, recycling, canned goods, spice racks, dry goods, dirty dishes, sacks of pet food, utensils, glassware, and bottles of medication. The rest is a warren of negative space, narrow pathways angling to back bedrooms and bathrooms. Staircases leading to upper bedrooms and basements are home to shoes, cases of soda and beer, bundles of toilet paper, tools, mops, buckets, books, and brimming laundry baskets.

For the elderly and disabled, water stacked anywhere other than in the kitchen requires many trips back and forth to retrieve one or two bottles at a time, working their way through a shrink-wrapped case too heavy to move on their own.

Cases of water, like breeding rabbits, can swamp a

dwelling in no time. The minimum weekly amount of water required depends on the number of people living under one roof. Summer heat doubles the need. No man is an island, except here—a people surrounded by water—John Donne, reduced to straight man.

SIX

A middle-aged man with red, rheumy eyes claims they've cut off his water, wants everything we can spare. He's keen to find his phone, bellows to a guy across the street, maybe did he leave it over there? He ducks into his house, reappears waving a thick, dog-eared folder stuffed with clippings, legal and medical documents. Says the water made him sick, hikes his pants to expose a discolored leg. Yanks his waistband down displaying mottled flesh below the beltline. Brandishing the found phone triumphant, he taps. Here's his interview with the *Detroit Free Press*. Swipes through photos taken at rallies, protests, and public meetings.

By now, media interest in Flint is waxing and waning with every fresh news cycle. A coppery Donald J. Trump announced his presidential bid from the bottom of a gilded escalator in Trump Tower nearly a year ago. The 2016 Republican National Convention will be held at Rocket Mortgage Field House in Cleveland in four short months. Only Trump, Senator Ted Cruz, and Governor John Kasich remain in the Republican race. In our semi-official-looking vests, sporting laminated badges, perhaps we represent one last, unpromising opportunity to capture the world's attention, if only for a moment, before the room is sucked dry of oxygen.

Evidence presented, he rests his case. We deliver our verdict—six cases of Aquafina—then wish him the best of luck, three of us inhaling diesel exhaust at the rear of the ERV. We have our instructions. The less time we spend at each stop, the more water we can distribute during our shift. How many thirsty people would it have cost to give the guy a few more minutes, read the interview, maybe watch a couple of videos? He recedes in my side view, passionately appealing his sentence alone in the middle of the street until I lose sight of him around the next corner.

EIGHT

Flint is a river town due south of Saginaw Bay, settled by fur traders, lumbermen, land speculators, and brokers of farm commodities, incorporated in 1855 to accommodate the needs of a vibrant carriage manufacturing trade, ballooning apace to support a nascent automobile industry. The local labor pool of the day was shallow—people of German and Scandinavian stock who had already found prosperity growing corn, silage, and sugar beets and raising livestock. Immigrants from European nations deemed less desirable, like Ireland, southern Italy, Poland, and new nations risen from the ashes of the Austro-Hungarian Empire, along with the offspring of former enslaved people fleeing Jim Crow, are wooed for their willingness to take the worst jobs for the shortest wages. Grateful for work, sufficiently constrained by a capricious social contract so as not to sink their teeth to deeply into the hand that fed them.

Industry and citizenry, like the first European settlers and the Ojibwa before them, drew Flint River water until 1967, when the city connected to the reliable but distant Detroit municipal water system. The river lends the city a disarming leer, a drunken grin plastered between the hangdog creases of the interstates. The ironic heart of the joke—abundant, clear flowing water drew the first humans. Today, the lack of safe water threatens continued human habitation. The damage took less than a lifetime. I cross the river several times a day, delivering water to people living near its banks. In some places it flows stunned through a barren concrete trough. Little houses on shaggy oxbows, Jon boats in yards, herald slower, cooler sections, shady and inviting on hot afternoons.

The river runs a shameful gauntlet, doomed to parade past what's left of this once vibrant city of hard-working union men and women. It mirrors the surviving edifices of the wealthy, long decamped, and the more modest dwellings of the forgotten and forsaken. The river leaves town quietly, wanders north to vanish into an indifferent Shiawassee, before quietly drowning itself in Saginaw Bay.

NINE

After weeks of stacking water in dining rooms, hallways, basements, garages, bedrooms, and bathrooms; under stairwells, behind couches, next to stoves and refrigerators; on counter tops, coffee tables and landings; outside, on screen porches, I'm still surprised to hear the hectoring chirp of a smoke detector with a dead battery. Chirping, common as brimming ashtrays, threadbare carpet, pungent cooking odors, pit bulls, crime bars, blaring televisions, and children rendered mute by our sudden, inexplicable presence in their living room. The first few times I state the obvious, as if any reminder were needed.

"My son's coming tomorrow."

"I called the landlord yesterday."

"Shit, I ain't even notice it no more."

I observed a few small rituals whenever I visited my mother in her final years. They required minimal effort, took less time than making toast, but satisfied a yearning in both of us for much more, desire subsumed for something considerably less, but much safer. Upon arrival, after a perfunctory embrace, before hauling in my bag, I would dutifully replace her furnace filter and put fresh batteries in the smoke alarms.

The AmeriCorps kids who volunteer with the Red Cross had, up until the water crisis, busied themselves installing residential smoke detectors throughout Flint. Now, their talents have been repurposed to install faucet filters. I don't know if replacing dead batteries remains part of their official duties. I learn to ignore the chirping, stepping around busted recliners, leaving a trail of bottled water down dim hallways, working quick, quick, back to the truck—on to the next stop.

TEN

It's not much of a plan. Drive to Flint. Present myself to the proper authorities. Lose myself in mindless, cleansing labor. The little research I've done confirms that the American Red Cross is the official portal for organized volunteer efforts in Flint, aside from the ad hoc efforts of churches and local service organizations. In the earliest days of the crisis, a ragtag army of citizens, city workers, law enforcement, and Michigan National Guard mobilized to distribute water and filters. The American Red Cross Flint chapter isn't too hard to find. It's on the I-69 service drive near downtown, just south of the University of Michigan-Flint campus. The Brutalist, seventies-era building is just up the road from a General Motors assembly plant and Sitdowners Memorial Park, commemorating the famous Flint Sit Down Strike. In the months before Christmas, 1936, a nascent United Auto Workers union froze auto production in Flint, winning legitimacy and wage and working condition concessions from General Motors. The strikers ushered in a national golden age of middle-class prosperity and job security. The strike united the racially and culturally diverse work force and their families behind a common cause. The BBC called it the "strike heard 'round the world." The company, supported by state and local government, opposed strikers with deadly force. A number of men were wounded by gunfire. President Roosevelt's intervention on the side of organized labor, and the tenacity of the strikers, eventually forced GM to recognize the UAW.

The half-life glow of all that socialist passion, the high drama of men and women putting their lives on the line for a just cause, is difficult to detect this morning. The parking lot adjacent to the chapter is busy with the coming and going of nondescript yellow Penske trucks. The surrounding neighborhood looks forlorn and abandoned. Traffic is light. Pedestrians, at least those unencumbered by shopping carts or bulging trash bags, are nonexistent.

I'm directed upstairs to a large conference room that appears to have been the locus of a great deal of recent activity, inexplicably ceased. Cases of soft drinks are stacked in corners. Empty pizza boxes overflow trash bins. Passed from person to person, I'm eventually assigned data entry duty, transcribing logistical data from field records into a database. The software is balky. My enthusiasm wanes. Teams of corporate volunteers in puffy down jackets and Gore-Tex boots tramp in, then tramp back out. Everything feels impromptu, a strange combination of urgency and ennui. Quickly tiring of data entry—it fails to measure up to the muscular narrative I created for myself on the trip north, stacking water in a sandbag chain, chaos swirling around me, desperate citizens clambering for their fair share—I flag down a woman who exudes authority. Soon, I'm on my way home, having passed the background check, fledgling Red Cross volunteer.

A week or two of online training, classroom CPR certification, day-long conference room seminar, and a road test around downtown Flint in a gleaming, late-model ERV, and I'm ready for my first day. I show up thirty minutes early equipped with a crisp new city map, stiff leather work gloves, and dawning awareness of my naïve assumptions about the city and this, its latest crisis. I arrive that first day expecting a bracing plunge into frenzied, ground zero-scale efforts to save the citizens of Flint. There's nothing about long-traumatized Flint this frigid morning, however, to suggest anything more urgent than a city waking to familiar trouble, hoping merely to survive until happy hour, choir practice, or *Wheel of Fortune*. I'm the newest team member in a stubborn grudge match destined to play itself out long after I've left the field.

ELEVEN

This neighborhood west of Dort Highway near Dewey Park is new to me, forlorn and desperate-looking even on a brilliant, sunny afternoon. I park in front of a modest ranch on a deserted residential street. Note a few boarded-up houses, parked cars in various states of disrepair, yards returning to meadow, baking planes of puckered shingles, cracked tongues of driveways speckled with empty water bottles. A street at once depopulated in aspect, but alive with flickers of life—a green hanging plant, a small pink bicycle tipped on its side, hum of window AC. *Pock. Pock. Pock.* Across the street sits a sprawling, well-kept ranch. Behind the house, dominating the backyard, a full-size tennis court simmers behind a high fence. An empty referee's chair hovers above a net post. A dignified older man in blinding tennis whites practices his serve, anti-freeze-colored balls glowing like pushpins on the large campaign map of the opposing court. The Sport of Kings, clinging to life in this post-industrial hinterland. *Pock. Pock.*

My father paid no attention to professional sports. Zero. Unlike other dads on the block, he didn't putter around the house on weekends with a cold Stroh's in his hand, listening to the Tigers on WJR. We never attended a game together. He installed a backboard on the garage, but I don't think I ever saw him shoot a free throw or recall him dunking on me. We made a half-hearted attempt once at a round of golf. I won't say we *never* played catch, but I don't think he owned a glove. The little I learned about the arcane rules of baseball … well, let's just say the finer points of the game still elude me. Therefore, it's difficult to imagine us playing something so intimate, so intensively competitive as singles tennis. Hard to picture us sharing so intentional a space as the green and red rectangles of a public court on a hot July afternoon, facing off across the eleventh commandment of the net. Impossible to see him, in my mind's eye, *run.*

The man has a relaxed, easy serve. I wave as I exit the ERV. He salutes me with a tip of his racket, dips into a wire ball caddy, form flawless, his spirit seeming to soar with every smash. I hope he finds a worthy opponent. Game, set, match.

TWELVE

A man loiters in front of his building a good distance from the street. I've called ahead to avoid having to drive around searching for the address in this sprawling warren of identical townhouses. Townhouse complex runs are the most difficult assignments, as we must navigate nondescript mazes designed to confound the casual driver and discourage those who don't belong. Residents approach idling ERVs expecting emergency relief, only to be told we are dispensing, well … emergency relief—with qualifications. Ostensibly, only those unable to independently access a water distribution site are eligible for water delivery. Who can blame them for asking? Emergency relief seems, after all, to be the mission as advertised. Such a system works far better in neighborhoods of single-family homes, where the whole transaction can take as little as five minutes. Scratch a DRV circling a townhouse complex of multi-family residences, and reveal dun-colored, low-level dread.

He needs ten cases. Apologizes profusely—his place is on the third floor. I stack six cases on the hand truck, my partner and the man carry two apiece, and off we go, parading across a parched expanse of weedy lot. We unload on the stoop, one case to prop open the door. My partner stays with the ERV while the man and I lug water up six flights. It's sweltering in the airless stairwell. The man pauses on the second-floor landing, coming back down. His breathing is shallow, color bad. I ask if he's okay. He nods, hands on knees, gasping for breath. I suggest he wait by his door while I bring up the remaining water. Task completed, the man thanks me, extends a hand. Both of us are winded and find it hard to talk. Does he share my sense of having experienced a rare moment of human connection stripped of artifice, momentarily free of the burden of presumption and mistrust acquired over a lifetime? Perhaps we're just dehydrated, a sip of water all we need to bring us around.

I take care to remove my damp, filthy work glove. Later, driving out of the complex, I spot him walking toward the rental office. I wave, but he seems not to notice, relaxed and at ease among a group of men, laughing among themselves at some private joke.

THIRTEEN

I knock for a minute or two, listen, knock again. Long minutes later, I hear muffled stirring upstairs. A large woman finally appears, flushed from the effort of having descended the stairs, instantly rendering petulant my impatience. She says she's recovering from hip surgery and hasn't had a delivery in over a week. She needs ten cases. We stack them down the hallway, leaving only a narrow pathway disappearing into gloom at the back of the house. Water-frescoed plaster sags overhead. She's eager to talk now that she's made the effort of answering the door. Two adult sons are asleep upstairs, one autistic, the other debilitated by head injury. I listen, frown, nod my concern. Having spent thirty years as a special educator, I'm familiar enough with the challenges she must face day in and day out that I'm rendered speechless. A sense of helplessness washes over me.

What will become of this woman and her sons? How will they manage, I wonder? Climbing back up the stairs will require fortitude, if not outright physical assistance. I find myself hanging, toes a hairbreadth off the ground, on the horns of a moral dilemma. Who to blame, goddammit. Men in power, the clockworks of the universe? If there's a God in heaven … and so forth.

On the way out, I wish her luck, remind her to *have a nice day*. It would be impossible to feel more ineffectual; a sense of fecklessness pooling about me as if my pants had suddenly dropped to the floor to the tune of "Stardust." I step into soft morning light caressed by a gentle breeze, endless blue sky overhead. A hallelujah chorus of forsythia erupts, yellow and shameless, serenading me loudly, mercilessly, as I slink back to the ERV.

FOURTEEN

My mother was the heart and soul of the family. If my father was the bringer-home of bacon, hand on the wrench that kept the cars running, oxygen thief—every room he entered depleted of air—she was constant as the Morning Star. The singer of songs, reciter of rhymes and maid of make-believe. We danced—to forty-fives, the radio—Bill Justice's "Raunchy," Hank Williams's "Kaliga," and the York Brothers' "Hamtramck Mama."

Hamtramck, Michigan. Encapsulated by the City of Detroit, urban beetle in amber. Historic gateway to immigrants from central and eastern Europe, Appalachia, the Ozarks, and, over time, the Middle East—late, from Africa and east Asia and pioneering suburban kids seeking cheap studio space. My parents took a flat on Caniff, near Joseph Campau Avenue, sharing a bathroom with an older Polish couple, the Geibors. Ornate Catholic churches, Polish social clubs, and unassuming shot-and-a-beer bars abounded. The sprawling Dodge Main plant dominated the neighborhood.

She may have fantasized about life as that latter song's free-spirited namesake. I remember her dancing and popping her fingers. She'd vamp, twirl around the room to Arlen and Mercer's "Blues In the Night"—probably the Rosemary Clooney version—pantomiming the chanteuse, thin dowel of a red Tinker Toy standing in for a saucy cigarette. She was a drop dead-ringer for Patsy Cline. They were the same age, Tennessee gals born eight days apart.

One night in 1963, she returned from Kresge's with a big surprise; a forty-five of "I Want To Hold Your Hand"—"I Saw Her Standing There" the B-side. I can still see the orange and yellow Capital swirl spinning hypnotically on the little turntable. We stood there for a moment, transfixed, my mother, brother, and me, stung by the sublime revelation of the Beatles. Once my father abandoned the field for the basement, we Twisted our asses off like Chubby Checker, lighting fresh Tinker Toys off the stubs of the old.

FIFTEEN

Over the weeks and months, I encounter more than a few people who have had their water cut off for not paying their monthly water bill. People who have no choice but to go on living in their home. I'm curious to know how they manage, maintain some minimum level of hygiene, let alone sanity, but dare not ask the question. Flint and Genessee County had some of the highest water rates in the state prior to the water crises. High rates levied by the Detroit system, coupled with an unfinished pipeline project from Lake Huron connecting to a new regional water treatment facility, contributed to the decision to draw water from the Flint River in the first place.

Everyone I speak with complains bitterly of the devil's bargain they've been handed—forced to pay high water and sewage rates in exchange for an essential service that dooms their children to a life sentence of brain damage, exposes everyone in the house to potentially fatal illness, and destroys the hard-won value of everything they have worked and sacrificed to achieve. Most pay, though they can ill afford the burden. Money for lead-tainted water means less money for things like food, rent, and prescription drugs. Never mind transportation, clothing, and cable. Medical care? Forget it. Various programs exist to help those in need. The governor pressures GM to reconnect with the municipal system, in order to bolster tax revenue. Revenues do, in fact, increase, but are woefully insufficient to pay the cost of replacing pipes system wide. The pipeline from Lake Huron is eventually completed, but Flint won't be granted representation on the Great Lakes Water Authority Board until 2019 .

Throughout the crisis, many continue to use water from the tap, run through commercial filters we hand out for free. Absolutely no one I speak with believes the free faucet filters are safe and effective. Boiling is a common, but ineffective practice, as are brief showers or sponge baths that limit exposure to toxins. Pets are at risk. Basic functions like brushing teeth, cleaning wounds, washing hair, doing laundry, washing dishes, keeping babies fresh, take on new, upsettingly onerous dimensions. Food preparation, of course, has been transformed into a tedious, time-consuming exercise in opening and emptying dozens of plastic bottles. Now and then we stop for coffee. I half convince myself that McDonald's is scrupulous in their water filtration regimen. I'm amazed, as the long, hot summer progresses, that Flint's residents don't resort to acts of civil disobedience or defiantly take to the streets to express their frustration and rage at their predicament. Attempts at mollification by the authorities, at this point, seem such an affront to dignity as to be morally indefensible.

SIXTEEN

For a couple of months, my time in Flint and summer vacation overlap. I regularly encounter children playing in homes or out in the yard, curious about these strangers stacking cases of water in their kitchen and living room. How to explain to a child that something so benign as tap water, so universal a symbol of growing up in these United States, a necessity everyone takes for granted, has been transformed into a dire threat, poison from the spigot, kitchen faucets malign and gleaming?

Everyday experiences are processed and stored in the brain as memory. Research suggests that trauma isn't integrated into memory at all, but lives on, ever present in the moment, locked within the body. In fifteen, twenty, thirty years, how will the water crisis be remembered by these children, grown to adulthood? How will they cope with neurological damage caused by exposure to toxic levels of lead? What about the cost to society? To taxpayers, saddled with the burden of underwriting an increased need for health care, mental health services, special education, law enforcement, and incarceration? In what ways will trauma betray these kids and reemerge flaring, filtered through the experience of having grown up in Flint?

SEVENTEEN

My partner today is a Flint native. Flynn is twenty years my junior. We've been delivering water in a neighborhood I've never visited before near Ophelia Bonner Park, a place that seems relatively calm by my lights. It takes Flynn less than a minute to firmly, politely, demolish my complacency.

"I never come over here. Is real bad, bro," he says, diphthong stretched to breaking.

A peeling nineteenth-century clapboard rooming house stands alone on a rubbish strewn lot tucked into the crooked elbow of an impenetrable thicket of bramble. I maneuver the ERV as close as I can. Ours is the only vehicle on the premises. The first floor looks deserted. Around back, a screen door bangs on a dank vestibule leading to a pitched, enclosed stairway clinging to the outside of the building, dark and forbidding, ending in a blind turn. Rather than lug water all the way to the top only to discover the place abandoned, we stand empty-handed peering up into the gloom. Ascending the stairs is second to the last thing I want to do, the last being look cowardly in front of Flynn. It doesn't occur to me that Flynn probably feels the same way. However, if one of us made a halfway convincing argument for leaving, I doubt he would encounter much of a protest.

"Red Cross water," I announce, my hollow voice a cross between a chipper *room service*, and an earnest *honey, I'm home*. Dead silence.

But someone registered an emergency water request to this address. It's stifling in the fetid vestibule. Add to that, the ERV idling, unattended on the far side of the building.

"Goddammit" I say, and up I go. The word hangs, hollow and melodramatic. I feel more than a little ridiculous, wish to retrieve it mid-air, certain Flynn's eyes are rolling in judgement.

From behind and below comes an emphatic *fuck it.* A moment later we're huddled together on the landing, eyes adjusting to the darkness. Four doors, all un-numbered, emerge in the gloom. We start knocking. A woman answers, the building's sole tenant. We restock her for the coming week, making several trips up and down the stairs. On the way to our next stop, I try to recall a light switch or ceiling fixture. Would I dare make that climb at night, turn that corner into abject darkness, deeper than the darkest coal mine? Despite having so recently and blithely taken the Lord's name in vain, blind faith alone, it occurs to me, radiates the only light of consequence when walking through the valley of the shadow.

EIGHTEEN

I taught public school for thirty years. My students—adolescents and adults—represented a wide spectrum of physical, mental, and emotional disabilities, compounded by economic hardship, dysfunctional families, mental illness, social ostracism, and economic disenfranchisement. They didn't teach professional distance at Wayne State University, but somehow I'd acquired it along the way. Boundaries exist for a reason.

There was the young man who registered frustration by bashing his head on tables and cinderblock walls. The young woman who expressed rage by throwing herself through plate glass. Young adults languishing, socially isolated once they were no longer eligible for public school services. All of them beneficiaries of my genuine, if circumscribed, concern, both professional and personal. There were, I'm sorry to admit, regrettable exceptions. I became *too invested,* as the poet said, in certain students. A breach of boundaries, however well intentioned, rarely did anyone any good, least of all the student. The prospect of salvation, if such a thing were possible beyond the exertions of lifeguards and first responders, may, at best, have little to offer beyond revealing the insecurities of the erstwhile savior.

The encounters I have with the citizens of Flint recall the formative years in my chosen helping profession. Every day is a struggle to balance empathy with the need to maintain professional distance, worried constantly I have too much of one, not enough of the other.

Nothing is so basic and good, so demonstratively beneficial, as delivering pure water to thirsty people. I always return to the

ERV, if not with a sense of having improved someone's life in any meaningful way, with the feeling that I am toiling on the right side of a river of betrayal and indifference. Absent lead-tainted water, people living in Flint would still be locked in a grinding war of attrition, a daily battle for survival, dignity, and some glimmer of hope. Insubstantial a presence as I am, in the greater scheme of things, the shadow of hopelessness recedes, perhaps for all of us, a sliver, every time I knock on a door and someone answers.

NINETEEN

The Garmin funnels us down this street a third time. It's hot as blazes, sun blinding, a glorious start to the long Fourth of July weekend. People sit in porch shade or stroll to and fro, drawn to the moribund commercial strip on Saginaw north of downtown. Payday lenders, check cashing joints, cellular phone kiosks, muffler shops, dialysis centers, storefront churches, liquor stores, and barber and beauty shops abound. We make small talk with a man who looks a qualified seventy. His small house is neat as a pin, yard tidy and trimmed. He retains the bearing of someone accustomed to having people cross to the other side of the street to avoid him. Take away the long, braided ponytail, web of tattoos, and leathery face, he could pass for a retired University of Michigan-Flint economics professor who keeps his hand in a weekly game of squash. We stack cases of water in his immaculate kitchen, admire his flowers, debate the likelihood of rain, curse the governor, exchange holiday pleasantries, then we're on our way.

I ease the ERV away from the curb while my partner records the required logistical data—case count, confirmation of filter usage and a current water test, number of filter refills delivered and brand. Accurate record keeping is essential to the mission of bringing water to Flint. Data, raw, run through a sieve and distilled into accountability and efficiency. I dislike intensely the tedium of keeping written records, and make a practice of handing the clipboard off to that day's partner. No one ever refuses. Some of them seem to enjoy the task immensely.

"Hey. Hey. *Hey, man*. I need me some disaster relief." I glance in the side view. "Could use me some relief, too."

We saw him on our first pass down the street. Thin, bandy-legged, he's loitering on the sidewalk, swollen pit on a rope lead. I park and exit the vehicle.

"Dog okay?" I ask.

"Nah, she won't do nuthin'."

"What do you need?"

"Ain't got no food, no water, no money."

His eyes dart and snap with high voltage, electrifying a maniacal grin. I'm wary. My instincts tell me to keep my eyes peeled for trouble. The dog is worrisome, but only half as much as its jittery owner. I open the doors at the rear of the truck, pull down four cases of Poland Springs, and make for the house. Except, I don't know which house is the right one. Both man and dog have vanished, having decided, on impulse, to inspect the interior of the ERV's cab.

The pit crowds my partner for space, pinning him against the passenger door. The engine idles. I pray the dog doesn't step on the column shift and engage the transmission. The man is pointing and laughing in the open door of the vehicle, casually holding the end of the rope. "She sure likes people," he says, with a reassuring giggle.

After a tense few minutes of cajoling, they retreat to a front porch. I stack their water next to them. We chat briefly. The guy turns out to be pretty friendly, in a speed freak, Neal Cassady sort of way. I wish him a pleasant holiday weekend and we're off once again. As we pull away, I glance in the mirror. "Neal" has donned a pair of glittering, outsize USA! novelty sunglasses. The dog looks roundly radiant, as if advertised in the web of some cunning spider. The man is mugging and waving a tiny American flag, an unhinged Uncle Sam. I wouldn't be surprised to hear Sousa, a brassy "Stars and Stripes Forever" booming from a bunting-covered gazebo, magically appeared amid the blight and ruin.

TWENTY

I take silent inventory of aluminum baseball bats and fireplace pokers stashed behind doors. Taped ax handles, fat ends of pool cues, and lengths of galvanized pipe. Tasers and padlocks secured to half-inch chain. Holstered revolvers. Pits and rottweilers, dobermans and German shepherds. I encounter few situations in which I feel personally threatened. Fewer still, residents who exhibit characteristic wariness or fear. People I meet seem to take the ever-present prospect of violence, random or otherwise, in stride. They live on an island, the dangers well known but part and parcel of life on an archipelago of poverty. On the proverbial launch back to the mainland, I often struggle to understand our remarkable ability to adapt to just about anything.

I have yet to see a shotgun, sawed-off or otherwise, but I scan the room every time. Distance and geometry are critical; triangulation of couch, hall closet, and front door, a critical equation. The spread, I'm told, allows for a comfortable margin of error.

TWENTY-ONE

I return to Tennessee to visit my ailing mother. It's late spring, 2014. I'm recovering from surgery on my Achilles tendon. Restrictions lifted, some residual swelling, I am able to depress the brake pedal, ease the limp when mindful. I'm alone, driving forward in time to where dogwoods blossom, tilted snow caps languish on the highest peaks of the Smokies, and morning mist blankets the hollows. At fifty-eight, I am gripped by yearning, urgent as the throb of a missing limb. Years will pass before I can fully articulate these long dormant feelings. In the morning, I wake to the sound of my own echo in her empty condo, slow to rise, alive to her presence.

Ima Nell was a pip, often declaring with pride that nothing seemed to bother me, referring to me, perversely, in the third person. She played piano by ear, sang in the church choir, instilled in me a love of music, if not musicianship. She was popular in high school, played basketball, was joiner of many clubs. Her photo was prominently featured in her yearbooks, a smiling girl having the time of her life. She was my fierce defender, much to my relief and chagrin, stepping in when I should have been standing my ground.

Gene had whisked her away from the life she wanted. I don't know if she resented him for it, but once he was gone, having observed a decent period of mourning, she smartly shed Florida and fled back to Tennessee, the place she'd always called home. The exact whereabouts of *home* confused me to no end as a child. Years later, in Florida exile, she took to writing letters composed at first on a manual typewriter, later on a computer. I never corresponded or kept them, chatty updates on weather, friends, and local bird activity lightly

51

skimmed and quickly forgotten. Coded declarations of love between the lines, unacknowledged and unremarked. I deeply regret the loss.

Taken randomly, my memories run from the pedestrian to things I'd rather forget. She was an early user of Facebook, accumulating a small village of "friends," reposting the cute, the cruel, and the inane. Once, I fainted dead away at her feet, mid-sentence, confessing to a date, my first, with a girl. One sultry summer day when I was about sixteen and she was in her early forties, we faced off alone across the kitchen table. I sat, silently enduring an angry dressing down, having come in late the night before. She railed, hair wild, barely restrained under a white elastic band setting off a deep mahogany tan. She smelled of Coppertone and wore her signature summer attire, a chlorine-faded brown bathing suit. The sight of her ample cleavage was unavoidable, my gaze frantic to land somewhere safe while avoiding the plunging scoop of her suit and her devastating glare. Furious, she dropped a strap and threatened to bare herself to me. The effect was luridly electric and queasily erotic, plunging us deep into Tennessee Williams territory. The sour shame of it stunned and confused me. Had we then the capacity to see—really *see.* If the veil of our defenses were to have suddenly dropped away, perhaps we would have glimpsed something essential and true and pure about our fractured relationship.

We traveled south on a Greyhound bus one summer in the mid-sixties, my mother, brother and me. My father couldn't afford to take time off work. The 600-mile journey took over twenty-four hours. The driver took special notice of her, cozying up at every stop, squinting through smoke from his Chesterfields, snaking an arm around her waist, issuing winking invitations to come ride up front with him. I made myself sick worrying about what this impulsive woman, this giddy girl, might do. I imagined disaster in spades should she abandon us for the smirking, hip-sprung Lothario in his ridiculous, quasi-airline-pilots' cap. I knew well the extent of her seductive power. I felt helpless, but also recall recognizing, maybe for the first time, her womanliness, an awareness that she was a person unto herself, an individual with opportunities, desires, and choices separate from mine.

We shared a great affinity for coffee and its comforting rituals. Ima Nell was well caffeinated throughout my childhood. Sleep came in brief lapses of vigilance throughout the long, lonely nights. Shared, as well, a shameless need for validation bestowed by others, a jigger too much oily self-regard floating atop a dark well of insecurity—a childish need for attention and approval.

She was ever hopeful, optimistic, and forward-looking. She always put past behind, and never looked back. Leaving home had toughened her up. She arrived in Michigan a lonely, fearful, fretful girl. She returned home a woman of grit and fortitude, exemplifying independent self-sufficiency. For her, the future was preordained, affording her a certain freedom. She eschewed the tiller, trusting the wind to bear her to safe harbor.

For the record, I'm here to spruce up the place for sale, shampoo the rug, survey what's left of the furniture. An umber-colored halo in the dining room recalls the table where once we sat drinking Folgers, gazing out on the feeders, recoiling from the bare hot wire of the past. I drive to Lowes for cleaning supplies. Seven hundred miles north, Flint water department employees perform the engineering operations necessary to begin drawing water from the Flint River. On April twenty-fifth, someone ceremoniously pushes a button, cell phone cameras flash and corrosive river water surges through city pipes and into residents' homes for the first time in almost fifty years, soft lead leaching into the life-sustaining flow.

TWENTY-TWO

I stack two cases of Meijer-brand bottled water next to six already arranged on the pitched, covered porch. An old woman sits in a straight-backed chair gazing out on the deserted street. She acknowledges our presence only long enough to establish her water needs, then retreats into silence. It's a beautiful day, but pointing this out seems exactly the wrong tack. She looks deceptively ancient, a weathered ebony figurine sculpted by hard work and adversity. Instead, I ask her about the pair of horseshoes embedded in her driveway near the sidewalk. In hindsight, I may have referred to them as "lucky." I hope not. Irony has its place, but it didn't that day, on that porch. If she suspected for one moment I'd spoken in earnest, she had every right to slap me.

She glances my way, expression betraying absolutely nothing.

"They was there when I moved in," she says, any residual luck, her tone implies, long since evaporated.

The shoes face outward, as if horse and rider had taken the time to carefully press charmed talisman into wet cement before fleeing for greener pastures—half-shod, but grateful to have made good their getaway.

TWENTY-THREE

The rough weave of Flint's near north side. I've been here enough to recognize subtle variations in the fabric, streets returning to wilderness, others vibrant and coursing with life. Almost every house on this block of small aluminum-sided ranches is spic and span in aspect. Lawns manicured, exteriors maintained to a fare-thee-well. We exit the truck and approach an older man, a GM retiree who says he's lived here over fifty years. He's taking a break from mowing. I get the impression lawn care is less a chore than arcane ritual, an essential element of a life carefully composed. I make my standard joke comparing his immaculate yard favorably to my own forlorn quarter-acre of dust and dandelions. This, despite lack of evidence anyone has ever found this even remotely funny.

He foregoes any pretense of humoring me, gestures broadly, sweeping hand encompassing the totality of lawns, shrubbery, and well-maintained facades.

"Folks around here keep their yards up."

His unspoken message? Behold, a display of collective pride; backs to the sea, it is here we make our final stand.

A taciturn man, he's seated, legs crossed at the knee, on an ancient, webbed patio chair, savoring a cigarette. He's wearing a crisp, billed UAW cap and white athletic shoes the size of matched Jacuzzi tubs. His striped polo shirt is tucked and immaculate, buttoned to the neck. Thin calves, encased in thin black socks with a colorful diamond pattern, disappear into voluminous salmon-colored slacks. He reminds me of my long-dead father, shadowy audience of one to whom I sometimes deliver tired, shopworn soliloquies from a bare, darkened stage to smattered, light applause.

TWENTY-FOUR

Ima Nell Nave grew up adored in the Depression-era, small-town South, her struggling father managing to spoil her on bluff and guile alone. She was pretty and vivacious. As a child, I would page through her dusty old high school yearbooks, trying to square the woman I knew with the tender bloom at the center of bunches of fresh-faced classmates. She drew people in with disarming ease. Lord knows, she loved the attention. She wasn't kooky and unconventional like Lucille Ball, but she could play the part.

With Gene gone much of the time, we are the sole inhabitants of our own little world; a dream come true for any small boy. She is fearful of the night, the flat Michigan landscape, the specter of loneliness. Suspicious of the neighbors, resentful she had been obliged to give up a clerical job in the heady heart of things downtown, angry at being left alone for days at a time with a needful, colicky child. Cosseted back home, sheltered from life's inevitable vagaries, she finds herself stranded on a deserted suburban island, her Friday, a fount of endless demands.

If I'm sensitive to the ever-shifting emotional weather in the house, it's not because I am exceptional, but simply because she and I are inseparable at a time when she is bereft of family and the company of other adults. We exist as a single entity, consciousness enmeshed one with the other. She shares fears and fantasies, frustrations and enthusiasms with me unfiltered. I am unwitting partner to a credulous, disenchanted girl grieving the loss of her old life. Gene is unable or unwilling to provide consolation or offer solace, permit himself the emotional surrender she craves. It is just the two of us, snug and more than a little beleaguered in our small, austere house during the long stretches between his unpredictable departures and returns. I am privy to everything, fretfully so. Her doubts and fears, obsessions and passions, prejudices and superstitions, bequeathed to me. The rudiments of her derailed dreams, with which to frame my world.

TWENTY-FIVE

As an ERV driver, I play host to a revolving cast of ride-along volunteers. Some of them are veterans of the drive-up, state-run distribution centers scattered throughout the city, where water is stored in secure structures adjacent to empty lots off major streets. During business hours, residents wheel in, present identification, and wait while someone loads their cars with cases of water, filters, and test kits. They drop off sample bottles of tap water for testing. The centers are manned by locals recruited from various community organizations, churches, and schools. The work doesn't pay much, and offers little in the way of intangible benefits. It's not uncommon to hear a veteran of one of these operations, almost always someone of my advanced age or close to it, complain about the lack of a work ethic among today's youth.

It goes something like this: They sit around in the shade, tappin' on their phones all day. They won't even get up when a car pulls in. They complain the cases are too heavy to lift into trunks; ain't enough shade; they're overworked. They don't show up. They disappear. They leave early. They curse. They're rude, or worse, indifferent. They won't listen.

And so forth. I find myself nodding in agreement, taking comfort in shared contempt for the lax work ethic of today's wayward youth. I suspect, however, the youth of today are no more or less motivated to work than we were at their age. The harsh denunciation of youthful sloth on which we old timers so readily agree could have easily applied to me at various times between the ages of fifteen and twenty-two. Conversely, the allure of common ground, a sense of solidarity, of a shared point of view, even one that betrays an undignified cantankerousness, is a mighty balm in hard times.

TWENTY-SIX

People often approach the ERV not so much for their own benefit, but on behalf of others. They sashay up to the driver's window, flag us down from moving cars, driveways, or front porches. They run us down on bicycles, intercept us in McDonald's parking lots. They appear, shadowed and featureless, in the bright square of daylight at the back of the ERV when I'm tidying the cargo bay, or stand patiently waiting as we exit a house.

"The old lady in that yellow house, she need her some water."

"Ain't nobody bring my grandmother water for two weeks."

"My father, he live over on Marengo."

Him: "My mother needs water and filters."

Me: "Where does she live?"

Him: "Where that bends parked."

Me: (looking) "Where?"

Him: (pointing) "Bends over there."

My brain associates *bend* with *river,* but the Flint runs well south of here. This goes on for some minutes, our Bud and Lou routine, before it finally sinks in. *Benz* as in *Mercedes.* Silver SL on the cul de sac—ahhh. Got it.

"The woman on the corner need her some water, but don't say it was me told you."

"Give me an extra six for the guy across the street, he don't drive no more."

"My grandmother can't get nobody to come out."

"Can you load a few in my trunk for my old man?"

A genuine sense of community prevails. Some stockpile water in garages or squirrel it away on sun porches. Some reside in houses with two cars parked in the drive or appear able-bodied enough, but hey—an extra case or two would ease things some. We make the effort to allocate resources fairly and equitably. Intimations of entitlement are rare; accusations of *working the system,* beside the point. After all, we are delivering bottled water to American citizens on US soil in the twenty-first century, an emergency caused by economic and environmental racism, human error, public indifference, and political hubris. The victims, a battered community barely surviving in the birthplace of venerable General Motors and sinewy union muscle, ghosts of a long-dead middle class haunting every byway.

TWENTY-SEVEN

Morning briefing in a windowless room in the East Bay Red Cross chapter headquarters in downtown Flint. I rifle a pile of reflective disaster relief vests looking for one that won't snag door handles and entangle me in the seat belt. AmeriCorps volunteers peer at phones, weak gusts of laughter from their table dying before infecting the room. Some are apple-cheeked, others brassy as plantains, collective features reminiscent of lightly bruised peaches. They come from Springfield, Mass., Sacramento, Calif., and Dover, Del. None will have heard of duty Sergeant Phil Esterhaus, salty character on the eighties cop show *Hill Street Blues*. "Hey, let's be safe out there," his once-famous tag line.

These kids drive box trucks, lug endless cases of water, install water filters, and take water samples. They darken the doors of scores of homes, flats, mobile homes, and apartments, many in very rough neighborhoods. They sign on for a ten-month tour of duty in various places across the country. This particular group has been in Flint for over a month.

"Be safe out there." The woman saying this is in charge of Red Cross disaster relief in Flint. "Stay sharp. If it doesn't feel right, drive away."

Last week, two kids narrowly avoided becoming bystanders to, or perhaps victims of, a shooting in broad daylight. "Your safety is our number one concern," she repeats. My partner today, a young woman from New Jersey, was the passenger in that truck.

"So, like we hear this pop, pop, pop. It was messed up."

Hunting for an address, the driver had funneled them into a scrum surrounding a man face down in the street. Blood on clothing, blood on concrete.

"Really messed with my head."

People in charge paired her with a qualified someone to listen, ask open-ended questions, validate feelings.

"Are you okay to go out?" I ask. She levels a flat gaze at the scenery, smoking cigarettes outside the ERV whenever conditions allow.

For the next few hours I scan the road ahead; take in entire blocks at a glance before committing to turns; listen intently, note every loitering pedestrian, register every passing car; every porch a vantage point—or an exposed position.

This street, is it safe? Are we safe here, right now?

Tomorrow, the AmeriCorps kids will be back act it, putting in another long, hot, potentially calamitous shift. I'll be elsewhere, miles away, carefree against the scrolling, primary colored background of a glorious summer day.

TWENTY-EIGHT

I drink coffee and listen to "Morning Edition." Crutches within easy reach, four-wheeled durable medical gizmo parked nearby. The dog sprawls at my feet, eyeing the hardware, willing a walk on leash. January 2016, and once again I am recovering from Achilles tendon surgery—left foot this time. Every day, Michigan Radio leads with the poisoning of the citizens of Flint. The news is dire and shocking, events fluid. I listen to the exhausted, overwhelmed pediatrician; rue the self-serving statements of a befuddled mayor and a stammering governor; chaff at damning evidence from University of Virginia scientists. State officials accuse the victims of political gamesmanship, a crisis manufactured by activist troublemakers opposed to a controversial emergency manager law. I feel hostage to slowly mending sutures. No bearing of weight for six to eight weeks. I'm nonplussed by the duplicity of the governor and legislature. My fury surprises and invigorates me, rage mounting by the day.

It is the dead of winter, over four months since her funeral, plenty of time for unhealthy rumination. How I relished the heft of the shovel that warm, sunny morning, standing at the lip of the grave, first measures of red clay drumming the lid of her casket. What I wouldn't give to relive the moment—claim the spade, lose myself in hard labor, backfill the hole myself. Jacket balled, sleeves rolled, shirt soaked, slipping and sliding in ridiculous shoes, I drive the spade home again and again and again. Tamp the red clay lozenge, fall sprawling on the grass, hands raw, heart hammering—spent, but cleansed. This same fantasy plays over and over again. I worry about intrusive thoughts; worry that I worry about them. When she was alive, calling her on the phone was a chore. These days, I reach for the phone with unhealthy frequency, lapses that leave me longing for a rapid pass to the hermit kingdom beyond cell service where she quietly resides in my imagination. Cursing the governor from the sidelines is futile. Wallowing in self-pity, pointless.

Goddammit. I'm fucking going to fucking Flint as soon as I can fucking drive.

Have I said this out loud?

The dog gathers herself, ears perked, head cocked.

TWENTY-NINE

Accoding to the Garmin, the house we're looking for should materialize through the driver's window … right … about … now. The yard surrounding the adjacent, boarded-up shell trails off into what looks like nothing more than vine- and bramble-choked vacant lot. But there, tucked into shaded gloom at the rear of the lot, stands a low building that looks to have once served the lesser needs of timber and rail interests. The woman who presumably made the emergency call stands in the barren dooryard. She must have seen the ERV, surely heard the friendly rooty-toot-toot of the horn. She executes a deft turn on forearm crutches, and makes for the open door, upper body supporting most of her weight, toes trailing crude calligraphy in the dust. Her hair is child's scribble done in fat, violet crayon, arms fleshy and tattooed. We've surprised her policing up her yard, empty water bottle tucked into her waistband, another clenched in her teeth.

Minutes later, we're chatting, three of us standing inside a dank, plank-floored room—sink, table, two chairs, vintage appliances, rusty metal shelving, tacked-on, brightly lit bedroom separated by a ratty beaded curtain. The walls are hung with dozens of tiny, hand-twisted gewgaws, miniature icons, candles everywhere—nineteenth-century occult trappings balanced against stacked cases of water and monastic deprivation.

She wants thirteen cases—*thirteen*, she insists, her date of birth and, of course, her lucky number. "You have a pretty healthy supply on hand," I say, cautioning against concentrating too much weight in one spot.

She shrugs, averts her eyes, smile like the *Mona Lisa*'s. We scatter eight cases around the room and prepare to leave. "Did you leave me thirteen, hon?" she says. Reminds us of her upcoming birthday.

Securing the hand truck in the rear of the ERV, I register the slow approach of a large, vintage sedan. The passenger, a man of indeterminate age, a character worthy of Tolkien, long gray pony tail, spade-sharp features, tall feather in the band of his leather cowboy hat, leans out the window.

"She okay?" Meaning, who the hell are you and what are you doing here?

A cottage deep in a wood, an eccentric woman branded by rumor, wolves on the prowl, and the woodcutter, true of heart, ax in hand, keeping an eye on things.

THIRTY

I navigate leafy, winding streets through a neighborhood of fine old homes set well back on deep, sloping lots. A landscaping crew manicures the wide, rolling lawn next door to the house we're looking for. A woman greets us at the top of a long, curving driveway, happily chatting with neighbors. She greets us warmly and says all she needs today is a replacement cartridge for her Brita filter. She could be a spry Pilates instructor for a Silver Foxes class at the Y, or a semi-retired, award-winning residential specialist in the bespoke Frankenmuth market. A UPS truck glides past. *Amazon Prime,* I say to myself.

No barred windows, debris, abandoned cars, burned-out shells, empty plats returning to woodlot. No knots of furtive men hovering like bees around the sweet pulp of liquor stores. The woman expresses sincere gratitude, then disappears into her lovely old Dutch colonial.

I'm rankled at having been dispatched to the far west side of town to deliver a single water filter to an apparently able-bodied, well-to-do matron, to the detriment of more deserving citizens on my regular beat. Never mind her pleasantness, or her resemblance to my late, cherished mother-in-law. The image of the UPS truck lingers. It only occurs to me later—the river is blind to our existence, even as it bends to our will on its endless downhill tumble. It binds together rich and poor, indifferent to variations of hue, tongue, or orientation. It coils like a snake around melting pot fables and mythological industrial juggernauts, indiscriminate on its long, wayward journey to the sea. Sure, the wealthy will weather the storm with weary smiles intact, more of an inconvenience for them. But who am I to judge who and who is not deserving? Everyone has a story to tell—the roller coaster ride of a company town—of thirst and hunger, the struggle to cleanse and cool. People as different from one another as the contents of your grandmother's button jar, united by an indifferent web of pipe.

THIRTY-ONE

The words "my father's house" resonate with New Testament vibrato, even lending themselves to the title of a Bruce Springsteen song. The memory of *my* father's house reverberates with the echo of his absence, my mother and I manning that lonely suburban outpost, forever awaiting his return, serial departures perpetually imminent. He takes to the road out of economic necessity, but is inclined to flight from an early age, never quite believing he is good enough, deserving of something as simple as a sense of belonging. He comes to resent, what must seem to him, our impenetrable bond, my mother and I. Perhaps he feels betrayed, fears irrelevance, anger hardening into spiteful forbearance. Driving home from Flint, tired, depleted, alone with my thoughts, he sometimes surfaces in pieces, flotsam in the wake of the wreck of the Hesperus.

He called me honey in the Southern way, Twain's term of endearment, the name Jim coos to Huck as they drift down the Mississippi. He worshipped and despised his own father as a martyr to forbearance. Despised himself for dismissing the poor man as hapless victim of a lifetime of bullying at the hands of a stern wife and her predatory family. He longed to play guitar like Chet Atkins. A six-string Sears "Silvertone" sat unused in a closet for years. I don't recall seeing him cradle it more than half a dozen times, remember hearing the sound of a single, strummed chord. It was decided I would learn to play in his stead, a dream of his I killed slowly, one discordant note at a time. His good humor was contagious. His nature, big-hearted and gregarious. Together, we watched Loony Toons, the antics of Foghorn Leghorn and Sylvester the Cat convulsing him with laughter that bordered on strangled, hysterical choking. I knew how to make him laugh, too. This seemed to please him and gave me great satisfaction. As long as he was laughing *with* me, I knew where I stood—not on the receiving end.

He sometimes mused about a different life, one of distant, solitary adventure described in books by Jack London and James Michener. He acquired a trove of camping gear yet never took us camping. He preached self-reliance, bridled at dependence of any kind. His union, the Teamsters, afforded us a comfortable middle class life but he had nothing but venom for their corruption and the quid pro quo of collective bargaining. A low opinion of his employer rivaled his dim view of the union in vehemence. A man named Bob Patterson, office flunky in charge of driver dispatch, suffered years of colorful, sometimes homicidal invective uttered around our kitchen table.

He had only to arch an eyebrow to send my heart soaring. Broadly, people were *hunkies* or *polacks, dagos* or *coons.* Individually, he treated everyone with kindness and respect. Purchasing a new car or boat was, for him, high-stakes poker. He was convinced all salesmen were slick shysters who took him for a rube, which only fueled his keen desire to possess the thing they were selling. Getting a good deal was tangible evidence of self-worth, vindication of every slight, real and imagined, he had ever suffered. He often referred to me, in the third person, as *kun-trary,* even though I was no more oppositional than an expired library card. I can't imagine what I did to warrant branding as a contrarian, but from a distance of sixty-odd years it sounds romantic, like being renowned a buccaneer.

I knew how to ingratiate myself with him, co-conspirators gleefully subverting mine and my mother's dignity and sense of self-worth. He was quick to support my decision to quit my first marriage. Was his surprising endorsement projection, unconscious celebration of freedom from entanglement? He could be chummy with other fathers in the neighborhood, or fellow boaters at the marina, but I recall no male friends of fraternal substance. He registered irritation succinctly with an arch "well, kiss my ass," punctuated by a theatrical casting away of the hands. He wasn't a drinker when I was growing up, but a cardiologist's remark about the relative health benefits of red wine put him on a late life regimen of Wild Irish Rose, a cloying wine of questionable value. He was good with a wrench, kept our cars in working order. In hillbilly fashion, a big fine car was emblematic of success, mark of the made man.

He gulped antacids by the handful, a large bottle of Tums ever-present on the nightstand. His job was not without stress, but hardly high stakes except on the worst of days. It was the road and something else that roiled his insides. He wasn't openly passionate but had great and enduring affection for my mother. Pressed, I would describe his feelings as paternalistic. He despised my fretful, sensitive nature. On vacation, he would pretend to abandon my dawdling toddler brother in parking lots, or thrust him unawares over safety barriers to dangle over rushing water, provocations that drove me to hysterics. His subsequent disgust with me was oppressive as a moist gout of heat ahead of a summer storm.

Once, enraged by my adolescent insolence, he had to visibly restrain himself from throttling me. I recall the odd desire for a good beating at his hands. A secondhand story had him declaring he would never allow me to go to Vietnam as a draftee, intuiting that my survival would depend solely on dumb luck rather than inherent cunning or skill. If the story is true, he never saw fit to share his conviction with me.

Hard Work was his middle name. Dogged and Perseverance, his first and last. He rarely missed work due to illness, taking whatever load the reviled Bob Patterson gave him. "I come to the garden alone while the dew is still on the roses," words to an old hymn he sometimes hummed, the song I requested be sung at his funeral. "He walks with me, and he talks with me, and he tells me I am his own"—it haunted me as a child. It haunts me still.

THIRTY-TWO

Flint sprawls undulating near the palm of Michigan's mitt. Neighborhoods on the west and north side are crisscrossed by streets that climb and wind, houses perched high above crumbling, sloping sidewalks. Access to such houses requires negotiating steep flights of concrete stairs leading up from the street. The views can't be beaten even in the most distressed neighborhoods. For all the calamity Flint has endured, spring through early autumn, it's a lush, leafy green city. Down at street level, however, gazing up at large, badly deteriorated houses, the ascent can appear daunting. One's sense of duty can waver. This is especially true near the end of a long, hot day humping water.

I sit in the ERV looking up at one such house. Only twelve cases of water remain from our third pallet of the day. Once they're gone, we can call it quits and return to chapter headquarters. Ancient stairs ascend in three flights ending at a run of rotting treads leading to a sagging, covered porch. A century of Michigan frost cycles has heaved the concrete into fun house misalignment. A solemn young girl answers the door. She watches silently as we announce ourselves, then vanishes into the gloom. Minutes go by. We hear sounds of concerted movement, the muffled *don't-bother-me-now* voice of an irritated woman, ganged footfalls.

Six children, none old enough to drive, emerge from the shuttered house; vibrant, incandescent kids cooped up on a beautiful spring afternoon. We descend to the ERV and begin unloading. The girl is already at work organizing her siblings into a bucket brigade extending back into the house. She is quietly, confidently efficient. The other kids follow her directions without hesitation. All are serious and slender, possessed of quiet dignity. Twelve heavy cases make their way to the top in good order. I take time to register each face in turn. Such lovely children, each one a prayer of hope and portrait of heart-rending despair. Watching them work in concert, their unsullied goodness in contrast to the stark landscape and my own trifling discomforts, causes my heart to swell and break. We wave our goodbyes and I coax a silent, feeble prayer up those crazy stairs.

THIRTY-THREE

Tennessee, late winter or early spring—who can tell—2015. A gauzy sky, the wooly backdrop to a steady, late morning rain. Islands of dark stains scattered across the expanse of oatmeal-colored, wall-to-wall carpet in my mother's condo resist my best efforts. It's work I welcome and wish to extend as long as possible. Once I'm finished, I'll have little recourse but to deliver myself into captivity, spending the remainder of the long afternoon and evening watching Fox News with my mother, her slyly insinuating caregiver, May, and May's malodorous dachshund, Tippy. Tomorrow, I plan to return home after a three-night, two-day stay. I console myself with thoughts of a late dinner at a forlorn chain restaurant and a glass or two of house red, before retreating to the cavernous condo, provided I can dodge the invitation to a home-cooked meal, sure to come.

Do we ever stop to consider, in moments of blinkered rumination, discrete elements of distant, portentous events quietly arranging themselves so as to overtake and envelop us at some unforeseen juncture up ahead? On my hands and knees in her barren living room, made emptier still by the lack of any visible touchstone with the past, I can see no further than my mystifying aversion to entanglement with my mother. I work the stiff-bristled brush in the manner of the desultory floor scrapers depicted in *Les raboteurs de parquet* by Gustave Caillebotte. Separated by hundreds of miles, I had long strived to extend the emotional distance even further by speaking dismissively of her to others. The unkind remark—another thousand miles. Grievance aired—ten thousand more. Mean-spirited ridicule—a hemisphere gained. Alone in her condo, her absence suddenly too big a mouthful to choke down, occluding my airway to the point of tears, I'm flooded with the feeling of distance instantly narrowed to the space between two adjoining musical notes. One note following the other, a tune recalled from childhood.

Hundreds of miles away in Flint, mothers prepare infant formula, children bathe and brush their teeth, the elderly take their medication and fathers boil elbow macaroni for their kid's lunch, none the wiser to impending danger. Those responsible will soon be confronted with murky evidence of their misdeeds and flatly deny responsibility—deny, in fact, the very existence of a problem. Maybe they're already weaving cover stories from whole cloth against revelations yet to come.

It will be another year and a half before my life converges with theirs in small, revelatory ways—for me, certainly not them. But on this particular rainy morning, the travails of Flint's residents are of no consequence, abstract as low pressure off the Canary Islands balling itself into a small, furious fist aimed at an unsuspecting Florida Keys.

I plan one more pass with the rented carpet cleaner, but before I can begin, my phone rings. It's May calling to report she is having trouble getting my mother from the recliner to the bathroom. Though conscious, Ima Nell isn't responding to her name or complying with simple requests. Normally, she is alert, engaged, and relentlessly upbeat, able to get around on a rolling walker and use the bathroom with May's help. When I arrived last night, she seemed fine. I drop what I'm doing and drive the ten miles to May's at top speed. I find my mother where I'd left her last evening, propped in her recliner, omnipresent television flicker reflected in her glasses. Awake but not speaking, in no apparent distress, she appears to have fallen under a benign, but formidable spell.

The problem in a nutshell—May cannot lift my mother alone. May and I, working in concert, cannot lift her safely.

Our mutually beneficial agreement with May is rendered instantly, irrevocably, null and void. Any peace of mind we may have derived from the arrangement, evaporated—May's supplemental monthly income, now in peril. I suddenly find myself stranded; my greatest fear, made manifest

I leave a message for the home health nurse, and settle in to wait. Has she suffered a stroke? Aneurysm? Seizure? Do I call 911? May counsels patience. For a moment, I suspect she is faking it to milk sympathy on the occasion of my visit. Panic floods in. Finding a new place with the level of care now necessary will take months and a good deal more money. We'll need the proceeds from the sale of her condo to finance specialized nursing care. Leaving tomorrow as planned would be tantamount to abandoning an eight-month-old to the care of a toddler in order to slip out for a tryst.

I'm visited, all at once, by a horrifying vision of the dark months to come—living in May's spare room, the never-ending days paying out slowly and with a sameness known only to convicts, monks, and costumed Disney actors in Orlando. Endless hours spent watching daytime television. Evenings, a brain-numbing carousel of *Wheel of Fortune*, Sean Hannity, Tucker Carlson, and local news.

I call my brother. "Don't panic," he says.

Easy for you, I think. Tippy snores on the couch, exuding the sweet, savory aroma of slow decomposition.

When the nurse calls, I describe mother's symptoms. She'll be there within the hour, she assures me. Mother's condition remains unchanged, a kind of benign, not altogether alarming, delirium. May passes the time by recounting her own laundry list of chronic health woes. Panic rises and expands floridly to encompass responsibility for my mother *and* her calculating caregiver. May cops to the disconcerting fantasy we are siblings of a sort, long-lost brother and sister, reunited around my—*our*—ailing mother. She radiates moist heat and smells of duct tape adhesive. Tippy reeks of end times. The local news anchor warns of a new phone scam targeting the elderly. The forecast calls for all night rain and, implicitly, nightmares I'll be helpless to forestall.

Vital signs good, the nurse can find no clinical explanation for her fugue. What's more, mother is beginning to rally. Before the nurse prepares to leave, she is able to stand and walk to the bathroom with assistance. Before long, she has fully regained herself, and May sets about boiling water, busying herself with dinner. I beg off and flee for the safety of the barren condo.

Two months later, my wife and I are visiting with my mother while May keeps a medical appointment. A trio of camo-clad hunters methodically gut a deer swinging from a tree in the yard next door. Strange. Can it be hunting season? On the cluttered table next to her recliner, hidden in plain sight amid a box of tissue, television remote, and hard candy, sits a large bottle of Oxycontin, "Ima Nell Hardin" printed on the label. May, I recall from our previous, impromptu confessional, has her own prescription for the ubiquitous opioid. I try to recall whether Oxycontin is on mother's list of medications. Did May mention anything before she left? Not surprisingly, mother claims ignorance of the bottle's contents and provenance. I enlighten her to the danger, only to find myself on the receiving end of her sudden wrath, old and familiar as a former tormentor turned up at the door with no place else to go.

I'd be surprised if the clang of the coin dropping isn't audible to the three sallow young men across the hollow, looking for all the world like extras from an episode of *Breaking Bad*. I feel certain they would giddily embrace the opportunity to avail themselves of a cache of pharmaceutical-grade narcotics so close at hand, so lightly guarded. She'd been high as William Burroughs that rainy Saturday, two months ago, my teetotaling, Baptist mother.

THIRTY-FOUR

t's hard to say whether the nineteenth-century structures in this neighborhood sprouted up around this small, block building or if another, even older building, had been razed to make room for it. The dimensions and architectural configuration suggest livery or coal bunker—obsolescence intentional and long pending. It is devoid of any distinguishing feature, flourish, or ornamental betrayal of human habitation. The sun is high, shadows in full retreat. The dusty gravel parking lot, at perpetual high tide, laps at the foundation, licks the threshold of the open door. Inside, visible through the windshield of the ERV, a young woman and a little girl sit on a small couch in a darkened studio apartment. Spartan doesn't quite capture the tableau. The woman says little, betrays less. We stack water next to a small fridge. The room is free of clutter, lending it an unearned aspect of tidiness. The lack of possessions suggests a budget motel room at check-out time. The absence of diversion is conspicuous. If the woman has a phone, it's not in evidence. There's no television or radio.

The little girl is immaculate—hair in braids, matching shirt and shorts, neat and clean. She practically glows, her silence deafening, magnifying her luminosity. We're in—we're out, her huge eyes tracking our every move. Her small hands clamp a conga-sized soft drink. Not once in the time we're there, does she relax her pinched embouchure grip on the straw or venture a smile around the hot pink length of bendy tubing. Why I am so unsettled by this isn't immediately clear to me. It could be the vaporous sense of transience, impermanence displacing the more substantial element of stability our weekly Red Cross presence would seem to signify. The woman and child appear poised to flee, the small, dark room nothing more than a glorified bus shelter.

Idling in the ERV, I try to imagine the sensation of tracking light and shadow across the room until darkness swallows the day, the world wizened and pinched within those four walls. I glimpse them as I pull out of the empty lot, side by side on the couch, gazing into the gloom.

Looking back, it was something about the young woman, herself. Alone, abandoned, forlorn, seething, unpredictable. Character elements I assigned to her with no more thought than pulling on a pair of pants. Unconsciously, presumptuously, I had associated her with my past, my mother, perhaps, even with myself, sending a chill down my spine.

THIRTY-FIVE

I run two cases of water to a house up the street. While I'm away from the ERV, a man approaches and addresses my young partner through the passenger window. We spotted him loitering in a yard as we pulled to the curb. The man registers a complaint of elbow pain due to excessive masturbation, then waits patiently for a medical opinion. He takes a moment to consider the wary young Samaritan's guarded prognosis, then wanders off, presumably weighing his treatment options before disappearing into a house a few doors down.

"He probably thought the ERV was an ambulance," I say. "Likely took us for paramedics."

The young man, a kid of twenty or so, laughs and shakes his head, returns to scrolling through Reddit on his smartphone. A case of Ice Mountain may not have eased the guy's pain, but certainly wouldn't have made matters worse.

Yeah, but I drink with this hand! Punchline to a sad joke lacking only a cringe-worthy setup. I give up after a few minutes.

THIRTY-SIX

Postwar economic migrants to Michigan, my parents eventually retire to Florida, leaving friends and family far behind. My father had managed, at last, to escape the messy business of belonging. Eternally restless, he's been a man in flight his entire life, pursued by some nameless something. Shame, rage, fear—perhaps all three? I'll never know. It hounded him to his grave, but not before wrapping me in its firm embrace, both of us hobbled by the past.

He lives his last ten years under gathering clouds of congestive heart failure and diabetes, his fate all but sealed. He insists on burial, not in Michigan or with his people in Tennessee, but in a soulless national cemetery for veterans in the blank middle of the Sunshine State. At his urging, my mother eventually returns to the place of her birth, the intervening years having erased nearly everything she'd once held dear. Beguiled by her as a child, wary of succumbing to her still-potent allure, I make little effort to convince her to return to Michigan, to her family. To me.

Family tragedy doesn't always explode, lashed to a brick hurled through the window. Sometimes it arrives parcel post, packaged in the most mundane arrangement of brown paper and twine.

THIRTY-SEVEN

This is the shortest parade I've ever been in. No marching bands, the ERV the only float—not a clown car in sight. Parade watchers abound, however, crammed onto a single front yard, the address we've been searching for. The truth is, I've been circling the block, trying to work up the nerve to pull to the curb in front of the ramshackle ranch fronted by a majestic willow, overgrown yews, and high grass. A group of men, more than enough for a rugby scrum, funeral cortege (including horn section and drum line), or old-fashioned barn raising, mill about, lounging on rickety lawn chairs, front porch, and the hood of a parked car. We've landed smack dab in the middle of a long, hot, afternoon smoker.

It reminds me, incongruously, of my father and his father drifting out to the yard after midday dinner. This would have been during the Kennedy administration, my grandfather laboring his final years as a tobacco farmer, our family on its annual two-week summer visit south. They are shaded by big, blowsy trees, which, possessed of the powers of speech, I'm certain would have drawled their vowels, laconic as the men sheltering under their spreading branches. Sitting side by side in a lazy circle of flaking, feathery, pea green Adirondacks, they while away the long afternoon. Throw a hand up at the occasional Fairlane or Bel Air headed to west to Maryville or south toward Gatlinburg and the national park.

I don't recall much in the way of conversation, unless their self-satisfied mix of pity and contempt for the fortunes of the town drunk, count. Clabo, first or last name, I never knew. Destined to wander dazed, up and down the county road, he wends his lopsided, grinning way to their shady glade, bums a smoke, and quizzes my father on life "up 'ere in Dee-troit." Bees buzz, air shimmers, menace floats, waiting for a call to arms or harmless discharge into the ether.

Then, as now, I'm wary of knots of men saddled with surplus time and lack of purpose. A timeless masculine quandary. Hitch up your britches and get to work or surrender to lassitude dangerous enough to make a Puritan cast around for someone to slap into stocks.

The idlers in Flint this afternoon run the gamut from young to old, nearly united in their preference for going shirtless on a hot, humid July afternoon. Beer is much in evidence, sweating cans of cheap suds or quart bottles of malt liquor. Almost everyone, to a man, fervently sucks on a name-brand smoke or cups a hand roll. A few venture welcoming waves or wan smiles. Our Red Cross vests and the ERV emblazoned with the universally recognized symbol for humanitarian relief negate the need for lengthy introductions. Anything less neutral than a businesslike "Red Cross water" seems ill-advised. I'm surprised when a well-built man strides up and offers to relieve me of the two cases weighing me down, bearing them, effortlessly, the rest of the way into the house. Soon, an amiable, if unsteady, gathering assembles at the back of the ERV. Many of the men live just up the block, or in the immediate neighborhood. We load up the car in the driveway, water intended for re-distribution at the driver's earliest convenience.

The moment isn't completely scripted, light comedy. Glancing around at the conclave, heady with testosterone, infused with alcohol, ennui, and exhaustion, it's hard not to notice the flat glares, a whiff of judgement passed—sentence pending.

I recall the pungent vapor of instability in the air that day, fifty-odd years ago in my grandfather's yard; Clabo, like my father, a war veteran. What drove him to the bottle, I cannot say. As to the possibility of old, lingering animosity, I haven't the slightest. My father had gambled on a better life in the north. Of my father's relationship with his own father, I suspect he idealized the man once he had distanced himself by escaping for good. My grandfather had endured a lifetime of tenant farmer servitude to his conniving father-in-law. It was the man's son, my grandfather's brother-in-law, who would one day lure my father away from home for good.

Perhaps my father struggled with a cascade of guilt and anger. I will never forget watching him stumble, blind with grief, from his father's open grave, keening, "He was a better man than me ... he was a better man ... he was better ... " He was seven years my junior that warm, rainy morning in 1983. I don't recall whether my mother comforted him in his anguish, though surely, she must have done. Shamefully, I stood by and said nothing. The moment is indelible, the only time I saw him lose control so utterly and completely. I had no way of knowing then, but I had caught a rare glimpse of the essence of the man.

Back in the ERV, the gathering of men—young, old, and in-between, somnolent or seething, disarming or dismissive—growing smaller in the rear-view mirror, I feel only relief. No denying the potential for trouble in the shade of those narcotic trees laced with buzzing bees. Men in numbers gathered to no discernable purpose—none I can detect, anyway—leave me twitchy. All that hair-trigger energy, coiled and ready. Roosting like strange birds of prey, colorful plumage on display, poised to take wing or flash talons at some secret signal.

THIRTY-EIGHT

ERV's are revered in the world of Red Cross disaster relief. Who hasn't seen images of them parked on flood-devasted streets, rolling past scoured concrete pads of homes demolished by wind and water, boxy symbols of hope amid the wrack and ruin, exhausted survivors and first responders waiting in orderly lines for food, water, clothing, and blankets. Piloting one through Flint, where the devastation extends back decades, owing as much to corporate greed, indifferent government, and institutional racism as contaminated water, it's difficult to discern exactly *which* disaster I am endeavoring to relieve.

They are specially designed to deliver and dispense hot meals, water, and essentials to people who have lost everything. They're equipped with exterior flood lights, siren, public address system, two-way radio, diamond-plate decking, a pass-through between cab and bay, cargo netting, tie-down ports, air compressor, auxiliary AC outlets, jump seats, interior work lights, rack and clamp systems for hot and cold food and beverage Cambros, overhead storage bins, dually wheels, heavy-duty diesel engines, bay drainage ports for hosing out accumulated gunk, and a swivel chair facing a sliding service window.

Delivering water in Flint requires employing none of these Swiss Army Knife frills. One shrink-wrapped pallet of water slides neatly between the wheel wells, enough room left over for a few loose cases of water distributed strategically around the bay. Remaining space is given over to boxes of PUR and Brita water filters and replacement cartridges, water test kits, water samples bound for the lab, boxed pitcher filters, recycling bags, and printed flyers of ever-changing state guidelines and Red Cross service delineations.

Only few weeks into the job, and I've grown strangely attached to my ERV. The vehicle has a presence, a gravitas that lends a sense of dignity to this miserable, man-made disaster. Prowling the mean streets of Flint, I am Hemingway behind the wheel of an ambulance in northern Italy in 1918. My *Papa* fantasy is, of course, so much self-aggrandizing, romanticized bullshit. The ERV doesn't ennoble me or the situation. People here want their goddamn tap water restored to what it was before. Short of that, they care not a jot about mode of delivery, my Walter Mitty daydreams, or the sage wisdom of my thoughts on Flint's misfortunes.

THIRTY-NINE

When I am twelve, my mother leaps from a stepladder into a neighbor's backyard, injuring her knee badly enough to require surgery and weeks of rehabilitation. I witness the performance, an impulsive act of bravado, a flagrant bid for attention. With him on the road days at a time, my younger brother a misperceived threat to my coveted sense of privilege, I claim responsibility for her care. I am thrown back in a swoon, bewildered and beguiled, to a time when Eden was ours, before the fall.

She mends slowly. I strive for approval. She basks in the attention. I chase a mirage of validation. Boundaries blur, and I feel myself vanishing into her circumscribed, needful world. By the time she's back on her feet, I've already fled, having escaped, at least for the time being, the pull of her gravity. I don't stop running until I discover, decades later, I've circled back, come up short at the very place I started, only a little farther north, just south of Saginaw.

FORTY

Banner-size photographic images, beautiful black-and-white portraits of two formidable looking women, are displayed in the front windows of an abandoned house. I muscle four cases of Ice Mountain to a woman living in the place next door. There are only a few houses left standing on this street. Few of these are inhabited. Lush undergrowth and saplings reclaim old foundation and sidewalk. I ask the woman about the striking images. Who are they—*were*? Who took the pictures? Who displayed them in the windows? Why? She says the house is scheduled to be torn down by the city.

"But, who are the women—do you know who they are?"

She retreats into the dim interior of her home, reply muffled as the door swings shut. I stand transfixed for a minute or two, then return to the ERV under their withering gaze. They follow me as I pull away, proud and unflinching, awaiting their fate with far more grace and defiance than I could ever muster.

FORTY-ONE

"The Mississippi Delta is shining like a National guitar." So sings Paul Simon in his song "Graceland." The river proper is shining no less brightly this morning, seen through my portside window in coach. It's 2017, many months after my time in Flint, and I'm flying to Houston, hard on the heels of Hurricane Harvey. Today is the second anniversary of my mother's death. A little over a year ago, I was delivering water in Flint. Last week, vacationing on Maryland's eastern shore, we tracked the storm as it howled up the Gulf of Mexico and made landfall in Texas. The storm scoured the windward islands, diminished, then revived with a vengeance over the warm waters of the Gulf.

My Red Cross Disaster Relief certification is still valid. I haven't volunteered for anything since my time in Flint, but the prospect of full-scale disaster deployment has niggled at my conscience ever since hanging up my DRV vest a year ago July last. I invested a great deal of time and effort to qualify as a DRV, and the Red Cross had invested scarce resources in me. Gazing west over the Chesapeake one evening, Foggy Bottom casting a cool LED glow on the horizon, I tell my wife I'm considering volunteering for Harvey. She has reservations. We both do. I realize I know very little about the deployment process in this, a more traditional, natural disaster situation, vastly different from the one I was familiar with in Flint.

I make some calls from Maryland. Within a day or two of returning home, I'm back in Flint at the Red Cross chapter HQ, squaring my paperwork, reactivating my status. It's quiet, almost deserted, parking lot nearly empty. It feels good to be back in Flint. I'm half-tempted to drive down

Dort, past the water treatment plant tower, but I don't want to spoil the memory.

Harvey is history by the time I receive my marching orders, airline voucher, expense debit card, identification badge, and no-nonsense, heavy duty DR vest. At one point, I'd been told to prepare to drive an ERV from Flint to Florida. Hours later, I was advised I'd be flying into South Carolina for deployment inland. Hours after that, I am slated for someplace along the Texas Gulf coast west of Galveston. But in the end, it's Houston for me, a place I've never been, in a state that has bewildered and fascinated me since long before Molly Ivins designated George W. Bush, "Shrub."

A group of us rendezvous late morning at George Bush International Airport. Someone has keys to a Red Cross authorized rental. Registration at Red Cross HQ in downtown Houston, a brief stop at my hotel to check in and drop off my bag, frantic team assembly back at HQ, and the next thing I know I'm being rushed southwest out of downtown Houston bound for my designated field kitchen. All is in flux. Teams are assembled, ad hoc. DRVs are mustering out, checking in. I'm paired with a woman in her late seventies, Betty, a talkative, feisty veteran of hurricanes, floods, and wildfires. Her spouse, retired military. They live near San Diego. Normally, they deploy together, but he has chosen to remain home to care for their dogs.

On my approach to George Bush International, nothing had appeared amiss. Descending, I noted some missing roofs, a smattering of blue tarps, a curious proliferation of ponds dotting the landscape, but vast stretches of standing flood water weren't apparent. On the ground, city center, my untrained eye detects nothing out of the ordinary, no evidence this area was so recently walloped by a Category 4 hurricane that brought record rainfall and caused significant loss of life and property.

Sugarland. The name of the sprawling suburb where my assignment is located. It's also the name of the megachurch hosting the field kitchen—Sugarland Baptist Church. Parking lot big enough to accommodate a decent-sized theme park, located right off the freeway, surrounded by malls and chain restaurants. ERVs are lined up around the perimeter in numbers I've never seen before. It's impossible not to associate Sugarland Field Kitchen with a military installation. I imagine rows of doughty Spitfires queued up on shiny, orca-black tarmac at some damp RAF base near Ipswitch in 1942, waiting for the cloud cover to lift.

Here in Houston, the sun boils in a cloudless sky. My phone reads ninety-four degrees Fahrenheit—in the shade. Betty and I are assigned an ERV and dispatched west to an area near a tiny town called Richmond. We're told to be on the lookout for a fish market, vague landmark proximate to a trailer park hard hit by flooding. Sugarland Field Kitchen has been in operation for less than two weeks. All the managers are from someplace else, as are most of the DRV's. No one seems to know, precisely, where the hardest hit areas are, or how best to get to them. I aim the ERV west and hope to hit our mark, or at least drop us inside the ball park.

Red Cross disaster deployments require a minimum two-week commitment. Understandable, given the cost of training, travel, housing, and the logistics of shuffling people in and out while keeping manpower at optimum levels. I arrive, prepared to sleep in a shelter, hoping to secure a cot, as I hadn't brought a sleeping bag. Red Cross authorities put me up at the Crowne Plaza Reliant near downtown. NRG Stadium—it takes me a day or two to figure out the acronym—is right across the street, next door to the shuttered Houston Astrodome. When did they board *that* place up?

The Crown Plaza Reliant suffered significant water damage. Navigating the hotel is like wandering the Large

Hadron Collider if it had been modeled on a wildly fanciful tarantula. After listening to tales of harrowing conditions from Red Cross volunteers working and sleeping in the massive shelter at NRG Stadium, I am grateful every time I meander lost in the hotel's moldy and mildewed hallways. Assigned my own ERV, I will return here late for the next twelve nights, making the daily ninety-minute round trip to Sugarland Field Kitchen.

After driving around aimlessly, we stumble on Richmond Trailer Park, hard by the dirty, penny-colored Brazos River, subdued within its banks. Judging by what's left of the park, Harvey set the river on a rampage that scooped out a great chunk of real estate, along with everything perched on top of it. We set up in the middle of the wrack and ruin and prepare to feed survivors. I walk from one end of the park to another, calling out to the people who remain, but get few takers. I don't speak Spanish, but there can be no doubt about our presence or purpose. Everyone is outdoors, under flimsy makeshift shade, surrounded by debris piles, mud, and uprooted trees. After leaving the trailer park, we drive around the area looking for hungry, thirsty people. I turn into a gated golf-course community of winding lanes intertwined with a serpentine watercourse. Mega-mansions, partially obscured behind towering debris piles of drywall, cabinetry, furniture, clothing, toys, electronics, appliances, carpet and padding, flooring, and other artifacts of modern American life, drift by. We feed a few more people, but, generally, most seem too focused on adding to the cairns to eat.

Two days later, we're assigned to the Braeswood subdivision southeast of downtown, situated in a crook of Brae's Bayou, essentially a gargantuan concrete drain that bisects the city west to east. The sub is hemmed in by busy thoroughfares on the other three sides. In the 1950s and 60s, the Army Corps of Engineers "channelized" Houston's myriad natural bayous, imposing order on the capillary flow of water through the swamp upon which the city is built. The residents of Braeswood, like those in Flint, are bound to the financial millstone of their property. One weary man put things in perspective for me one evening, chatting next to the ERV. He humors me for a moment or two, a patient smile for my sincere expression of sympathy for his loss. We gaze at his ruined brick ranch, turned inside out, organs and entrails piled high in the street.

"This our third flood in five years," he says. "We got almost as much rain on Memorial Day, 2015. Then we got hit with Tropical Storm Bill." That much rain, in such a short span of time, swells Braes Bayou, rendering the concrete breadth of the man-made channel laughably puny. Crews are already razing homes closest to the bayou. Residents north of the bayou, at the greatest distance from the concrete lip, escape serious flooding. The largely working-class Latino residents living in Braeswood were able to afford the tidy brick ranches on good-sized lots with mature trees, precisely because of the development's proximity to the bayou.

I spend the remainder of my time in Houston feeding and hydrating the residents of Braeswood—midday meal and dinner—repeat. Protein, starch, and a vegetable. Water, snacks, and MRE's. Some have chosen to remain in their homes. Others spend the day stripping their house down to the studs, dragging spent to a shelter or motel at night. Generator hum accompanies our choreographed efforts as we serve the last few dinners, well after dusk. An ancient woman in a floral caftan serenades us in Spanish, two shows a day. The days themselves are scorchers, humidity building but never breaking. Unlike Flint, our … what? Clients, people in need, disaster victims, come to *us*, line up at the ERV for assistance. There's just enough time for a brief word, expression of condolence, shared wry joke or a bit of gallows humor.

We crawl slowly up and down the streets, stopping every fifty yards or so. I announce *almuerzo caliente*, and *cena caliente*, and *agua*, over and over again on the PA, in laughable Spanish. Bedraggled, dazed, in shock, pinballing between the seven stages of grief, they queue up. I pass clamshell after clamshell through the window, but feel at a distinct remove from the souls outside the ERV. The scenes are heart-rending, but the job requires focus, organization, and a certain amount of detachment.

In Flint, I encountered people in their homes and on the street, contaminated water only the latest in a long line of insults, foreshadowing more to come. The devastation, no less acute than what Harvey visited on Houston, was folded into the community's long, extended spiral of decline. Houston would rebuild. The poor would still take the brunt of future storms, of course, but didn't seem burdened with the perception they had somehow brought calamity on themselves; like ill-trained children who had misgoverned their city, requiring the state to step in. I felt a certain kinship with the people I met in Flint. I can picture myself squinting under a showerhead, trying not to let water run into my eyes and mouth. Seething at years of inaction and marginalization. What happened in Flint was a disaster. Making it right is in everyone's interest.

In the years since my mother's death, I often dream of water, in torrents or trickles. Vast bodies ruled by the horizon or placid, sheltered azure lagoons. Full immersion or a desperate race to plug a leak. It symbolizes persistence—water will find a way. It might have something to do with fear of letting go, surrender to inundation. Or possibly, desire for same. I would have to get back to you on this.

Flint, Michigan—a city once blessed with proximity to unlimited amounts of the water in a state surrounded by the stuff, chosen as habitable by those first humans for its river bounty—can't even count on a tumbler's worth that isn't beyond suspicion. Houston, Texas—sprawling megalopolis, thrumming engine of capital, risen from swampland, awash in oil—hard by a rising sea. Water finds a way.

FORTY-TWO

The ERV kisses the curb, an ungainly tub lurching to mooring. The homeowner stands in his driveway sporting a wide grin, steaming cup of coffee a hedge against cold drizzle. We review the weather, recap a mild winter, and prognosticate spring. He is a finish carpenter and proud Flint booster. His aluminum-sided ranch has been home for over forty years; kids long gone, wife chronically ill. Would we care to admire his handiwork?

The finished basement has a low ceiling and a snug feel I attribute to intentional lighting and sound-deadening tile. If this were a neighborhood watering hole and past five o'clock, I would order a glass of cab and settle in for a long, agreeable evening. The copper-clad wet bar reflects faux Tiffany gleam. Seductive glassware and liquor bottles vibrate in sunset glow on the backlit bar. A gaming table rubs elbows with a billiards table. Foosball near the bathroom; an enormous flat-screen television presiding over all. I admire fit and finish—molding, tile work, hardware, fixtures, hidden details revealed to us with a flourish. How long have we been down here? Inclement weather, a warm and gregarious host, burnishing light; it wouldn't take much to convince me to sink into the plush banquette, shake off the day and wait for happy hour to commence. A labor of love, a city down for the count and a man possessed of indefatigable faith and sense of belonging. A man fortunate enough to know his place in the world, to appreciate that sometimes, home is enough.

FORTY-THREE

Time to go, water delivered, a schedule to keep. We engage in a little chit-chat edging toward the front door with a man in his late forties. Fit, intense—owner of two angry mixed-breed dogs barking nonstop from crates in the dining room. He ushers us into the living room, wants to show us his set up. Desktop, laptops, video equipment, monitors, cords, keyboards, cables, mics, hard and soft cases. I scan everything quickly, components that may or may not be functionally integrated and operational.

"Check it out, brah." Claims he's streaming the whole deal from right here, ground zero, nerve center of this whole debacle. "Been doin', since all this shit went down." He shifts his weight from one foot to the other, bounces on the balls of his feet, flexes his hands. "Puttin' it out there, man. Coverin' meetin's, know what I'm sayin'? Recordin' interviews, uploadin' video and shit."

"Great," I say through a frozen smile, "but we really hafta' go. More stops to make." My partner, an exceedingly patient woman, listens attentively. The man paces, gestures, voice rising. Dogs bark. The ERV idles at the curb.

"Next time you here, we do an interview. Get into it, know what I'm sayin'?" Confides that he can read people. "Got *real* good at it in prison. I can read you right now."

The conversation has taken an unanticipated and uncomfortable turn. He's onto me, I fear, but am unclear as to how, exactly. His claim may well be true, but I don't consider it evidence of any extraordinary perceptual gift. "Even the dogs want us to leave," I say, trying to lighten the mood.

He gestures toward the street. "See that shit, man?" Only a few inhabited houses remain. Empty lots and blackened shells dominate. This had once been a comfortable, middle-class enclave, the West Pulaski neighborhood. I can easily imagine kids playing homerun in the street under overarching trees. Women exchanging gossip from the porch with mothers pushing strollers down the sidewalk. Men drinking beer on stoops, listening to Ernie Harwell on thick August evenings. Neighbors leaning on snow shovels, catching their breath, discussing the pros and cons of the latest Big Three pattern contract.

"You think they gonna run new pipe where ain't nobody livin'? Sheeit."

Tone accusatory, countenance gone dark, but the man has a point. It's not hard to picture the surrounding grid reverted to open country dotted with a few scattered trees and sentinel hydrants keeping watch over returning wildlife. Before we leave, he hands us each his business card, invites us to call if we think of something to say on the record. When not streaming righteous rage and indignation, he's available to DJ events, large and small.

FORTY-FOUR

In Flint, 2015 begins with public meetings to address the emerging water quality complaints of its citizens. One by one, they approach the microphone displaying bottles of discolored water, complain of foul odor and rancid taste, bewildered children in tow. With events in Flint unfolding all but unnoticed by the national press, I depart for Tennessee again, this time with a sense of urgency and foreboding. I had received the dreaded late-night phone call we all fear. The one that comes well after midnight, piercing as a klaxon. Ima Nell is bleeding internally, some sort of life-threatening intestinal blockage. She is still living with May, but I suspect that her time there has come to an end, one way or another. Surgery is scheduled for late that afternoon. If I'm lucky, I can make the drive in under nine hours.

I stop only for gas and bathroom breaks. To pass the time, I write a one-act in my head, a drama with comedic flourishes, a mother and son lost at sea in a leaky boat. The staging is bare, flats amateurishly painted, choreography lurching. They dance around the issues, evade the truth, remark on the weather. The son bails with disarming wit. The mother, by turns all wide-eyed innocence or canny as a pawn broker, oar cocked at the ready to deliver a blow. A climax eludes me, but I am keen to arrive in time to hear the surgeon deliver the denouement, applaud as he exits stage left from the pummeling light of the timeless waiting room, back through the sepulcher chill of the operating theater.

The surgery is a success, of sorts, prolonging her life another eight months. The surgeon removed most of her small intestine. Her time with May is indeed, over. I spend the next couple of weeks securing a bed in a local nursing home attached to the hospital. It's a small facility, the place where her own mother lived for a time before she died. The transition goes smoothly. Big windows give out on Mount La Conte, highest peak in the Smokies. She seems glad to be here. I won't call it premonition, but I have a strong sense this is the anteroom for her final engagement.

FORTY-FIVE

The young man riding shotgun hasn't volunteered more than five words all morning and seems reluctant to make eye contact. Jason proves unwilling or unable to act of his own volition, waiting for me to throw open the bay doors at the rear of the ERV and begin pulling down cases of water before making a move to exit the vehicle, sometimes not without my express invitation. Unlike other young volunteers with whom I've shared delivery duties, I discover right off the bat that I can't prevail on him to program the GPS for me or, like some of the others, quickly map the day's route on his smartphone. After weeks of navigating the city, the geography of the greater Flint metropolitan area, as well as the salient features of GPS itself, still confound me. Debasing myself as a technological hopeless case usually does the trick with the younger set.

Jason is pleasant enough. He answers my anodyne *let's-get-acquainted, but-not-too-much* questions perfunctorily, without any hint of hostility or reciprocity. He hasn't made any unreasonable radio station demands and seems at peace with my unspoken no-AC policy. I have yet to determine Jason's motivation for volunteering. Altruism? Padding a college admission application? Moral or legal conviction? Rigid fascination with emergency vehicles? Whatever his reasons, Jason is in no hurry to divulge them to me.

We settle into agreeable silence, despite my inquisitive nature and innate need to disarm others preemptively by winning them over—that, and conversation, no matter how mundane, makes the time go by quicker. After delivering a week's supply of Crystal Geyser to a house on a narrow, dead-end street running between deep drainage ditches, I find turning the ERV around is going to be a much trickier maneuver than I'd bargained for.

Enlivening our predicament, at least for the suddenly aroused Jason, is a Flint Police cruiser idling at the corner. I manage to angle the ERV in such a way that one final, short reverse nudge should allow us to ease forward, exit the cul-de-sac, and get on with our day. With only two beeps of the back-up alarm elapsed, however, we're jarred to the bone by the force of a collision with some immovable object in our rear. Jason is out of the ERV in a heartbeat. I've backed into a tree, the damage confined to the already battered, dirt-shedding, drop-down step hinged underneath the lip of the cargo bay. I half expect a dutiful Jason to make a citizen's arrest—report the accident to the cop sitting not fifty feet away, fingering me the perp. I make a show of inspecting the damage and exhibit what I hope is a requisite degree of regret and remorse, enough to satisfy Jason.

For the remainder of the day, Jason gazes out the window, and—am I imagining this—keeps his distance when we're out of the truck making deliveries. From time to time, he mutters nonsequiturs. "Bumper sure is bent" or "really whacked that tree," delivered with a heavy sigh of resignation. "Man, did you hit it hard, or what?" I'm beginning to feel as though I've been captured on CCTV swerving to clip a Leader Dog and its owner. At the water warehouse waiting to reload, Jason examines the damage like a thoracic surgeon probing a gunshot wound. When we return to the East Central Bay Red Cross HQ at days end, I race to beat him into the building in order to turn myself in, report my own negligence, deprive him of that satisfaction.

FORTY-SIX

My second-grade teacher alerted my mother that I was having trouble seeing the board. If they hadn't already noticed signs of near-sightedness, my clumsiness and lack of coordination had certainly drawn my parents' attention. This was the same teacher who observed that I suffered from a certain dreaminess and often sat gazing out the window for long periods of time, oblivious to the hubbub swirling around me. Perhaps I was lost in a make-believe world, a landscape through which I moved with the easy grace and self-possession of a center fielder. A world from which I didn't feel the need to conceal myself.

Vision corrected with thick glass lenses set in heavy black frames, my parents continued to remark unfavorably on my lack of physical coordination—*backwardness,* their preferred adjective. Iron-on knee patches on the outside of my dungarees, dubious merit badges earned for frequent falls. My mother somehow obtained a referral to a Mt. Clemens kinesthesiologist, a medical discipline with which she would have been wholly unfamiliar.

The day of the appointment, I recall a descending cloud of unspoken gloom and dread. The clinic was located in a snug little house on a pleasant, leafy city street in the county seat. The kindly doctor sized me up, the passing years weathering the memory to Norman Rockwell patina. My mother, in hindsight, fretted and fought back Goya-black despair. Shooting hoops and playing catch were the doctor's prescribed remedies; I don't recall hearing a diagnosis. We drove home, my mother beside herself behind the wheel. When another driver cut her off, she exploded in fury, cursing the guy through the open window, hair wild and flying. The image remains vividly explosive, decades on.

How to explain her anxiety and dread—such fury, unleashed? Genuine concern for my well-being, certainly. It's likely she didn't fully understand the doctor's explanation for my clumsiness and succumbed to her worst fears. Polio, a brain tumor, demonic possession; anything was possible. The other explanation? The doctor had unknowingly confirmed, clinically, definitively, once and for all, my father's long-standing accusation that she had indeed, beyond the shadow of a doubt, *ruined* me. What parent wouldn't be knocked off their game, to receive such news?

Perhaps we were both victims of some original sin, the two of us damaged beyond repair, subject to my father's caprice and casual contempt. I went on to shoot my fair share of free-throws and a respectable number of lay-ups, even seeing the ball through the hoop on occasion. To this day, I love the simplicity, rhythm, and concentration of a game of catch. Watching Kevin Costner's Ray Kinsella toss a few with Dwier Brown's John Kinsella, his father, in *Field of Dreams,* jerks a knot in my throat to this day. But no miracle cure was forthcoming. Rather, she and I learned to maneuver around him, dance circles 'round the maypole until we vanished, disappearing deep into our own sad grooves.

FORTY-SEVEN

I drive established routes, revisit the homes of those who lack access to one of the state-run water distribution sites scattered throughout Flint. Other days, I respond to a hot sheet of emergency requests for water, filters, or filter replacements. Routes change constantly, the hot sheet never ending. There are things to recommend about both modes of service. Driving an established route is efficient. It is possible to deliver water to the greatest number of people in a single day. One learns the route, a comforting familiarity takes hold, human connections are made. Working off a hot sheet, however, is a great way to see the entire city, crisscrossing and backtracking, never sure what surprises await around the next corner. There's a sense of urgency to it that heightens feelings of personal reward and magnifies perceived risk. Then again, I may be romanticizing a mundane, routine sort of job that needs no adornment.

The ERV's long whip aerial lashes overhanging trees, boxes shift and tumble in the bay, diesel left idling through every stop, door storage pockets stuffed with coffee-stained maps from long-forgotten disasters. I lug two, sometimes three cases at a time, or roll them seven-high stacked on a hand truck, everything fed through the open bay doors. The work is repetitive and endless; anticipation of meeting someone new at each subsequent stop, a source of welcome excitement. A delight to make a return visit, see a familiar face. Surprising, the number of people who invite us in, willingly, warmly, our arrival unscheduled, often at inconvenient times of the day.

The first thing I learn—identify yourself and state your business, delivered in a loud, sing-song as one bounds up the front stairs: "Red Cross water."

FORTY-NINE

The pie-shaped wall running up the staircase to the family's second-floor living quarters is gallery space for artwork made by a young person, someone much loved and cherished. I was here a few weeks ago, but didn't take time to fully appreciate the many drawings and sketches. Portrait and still-life, landscape and dreamlike flights of fancy done in charcoal, pencil, acrylic, and pastel. It all seems to be the work of one hand. The kid's got talent. But now, on my second visit, I notice the paper is yellow with exposure to sunlight, the vibrancy of the colors leaching away. On my way back down, I linger in front of what I assume is a self-portrait in charcoal. The composition has been rendered with confidence and is emotionally compelling.

The homeowner, a woman, is friendly, but seems weary and guarded. Who wouldn't be? I'm an interloper, here under a fraught pretext perpetrated by forces beyond her control. These pictures have been hanging for a long time. I am curious about the artist. Are there other children? Is the best of the lot in a portfolio someplace? Did he graduate and go on to study art on a scholarship at the College for Creative Studies in Detroit? The Rhode Island School of Design? Why only curated art work to the exclusion of family photos or commercial prints? Is he still making art? I realize, suddenly, that I don't want to know the answers to any of these questions. Memorials speak volumes, so we won't have to.

I'm reminded of the sweaty hot dog vendors of my youth at Tiger Stadium, or the Twin Pines guy who delivered dairy to our backdoor milk chute. Whereas, a salesperson, Jehovah's Witness, or pale teen come to squire your daughter to the prom will ring the bell or discretely paw the screen, loudly announcing your presence declares formalities are wholly unnecessary and to be dispensed with. There's something inherently intrusive or presumptive about it—smacks of the rarified world of the gloved doctor, rounding third, heading for home before you can register "you might feel some pressure here."

I try to remember not to step out from behind the ERV into oncoming traffic, remember to set the brake, turn on the flashers, lock the doors when we range wide, servicing multi-family housing complexes, keep accurate records at each stop. I develop the habit of listening to Paul Simon's *You're the One* on repeat, on my seventy-minute commute to Flint. It's an upbeat album, the late Vincent Nguini's shimmering guitar, Simon's knowing, unabashedly American sensibility over world music rhythms. It won't occur to me until much later, the complexities of love, devotion, and mortality sketched in the song "Darling Lorraine" spoke, albeit obliquely, of my mother and I.

I enjoy my time in Flint immensely and recall the experience with great fondness. Sometimes I get the urge to go back, cruise MLK on a sunny spring day, windows down, familiar landmarks scrolling by. See if I can remember the old routes, cruise the crumbling grid with a cooler of Poland Springs in the back, maybe spot someone I recognize, work up the nerve to stand on a familiar porch. Discretely ring a bell or two. Chant "Red Cross water," for old times sake.

FORTY-EIGHT

Bottled water snobs claim a level of discernment I've never experienced firsthand. Water, despite the millions in marketing dollars spent, is just plain old water as far as I'm concerned. I concede that additives cloud the issue; vitamins, caffeine, minerals, electrolytes, and carbon dioxide chief among them. Like the old UAW bumper stickers that proclaimed "I drive what I build," when delivering water in Flint, I drink whatever happens to be on the truck. Bottles and bottles of it. I am surprised, therefore, when someone inquires as to the brand of water on the menu that day. I've stopped paying attention to brand altogether, as an endless succession of pallets are tucked neatly into the back of the ERV.

"What kind you got today?" More often than not, this sends me jogging back to the ERV for confirmation. I've had people decline a particular brand, having already muscled two cases up from the street.

"Crystal Geyser, ma'am," a lesser brand in the eyes of some.

"Do you have any of that Dasani?" The answer, written on my face, she ventures, "Aquafina?"

"No, just Crystal Geyser. Sorry."

No one ever asks about the infamous "Diddy Water," Sean "P Diddy" Combs's entry in the lucrative water market, for which I'm grateful. The bounty of brands available are owned by just a handful of multinationals, happily pumping regional aquifers bone dry, paying little or nothing for the clear, tasteless raw material beyond nominal fees funneled to states and municipalities.

Funny thing is, after sampling everything that comes through the warehouse, I begin to discern subtle differences between brands. Evian—mineral forward. Kirkland has a l of sodium and activated charcoal. Crystal Geyser—do I det notes of kaolin and calcium carbonate? My personal favori Poland Spring. I like the jaunty label and associate it favorab for some reason, with that large, flat eastern European natio rather than the small town in upstate Maine, home to th original spring.

FIFTY

Same as last time, and the time before that: muscular pit chained and pacing in front of the house, empty driveway, no car on the street. We wait in the ERV for a slight young man to secure the dog so we can approach safely. We're responding to hot sheet, emergency calls. Once the pit is out of the way, we exit the vehicle, walk to the side entrance, and ascend the rickety steps. Through the open door, we spy a cache of water stacked chest high in a utility room off the kitchen. The young man delivers a mechanical response to what is, by now, a perfunctory question.

"Momma wants four cases of water." He's probably in his late teens, black-framed glasses askew on a handsome face. He avoids eye contact, says almost nothing. His mother makes the emergency calls, but is never home when we arrive. She hasn't registered for regular route service. The emergency calls continue. I detect mild cognitive impairment and a strong undercurrent of fear and mistrust. The pit is less companion than trip wire.

I knew I'd lost my audience on our first visit when I tried to explain Red Cross emergency protocol. If we leave no water, he will blame himself, store mounting fear and guilt against his mother's return. Maybe she works one, two, or three part-time jobs, gets too little sleep. Perhaps she frets about leaving him alone so much. Suffers the exquisite guilt reserved for the parent of a special-needs child. As we drive away I pray the joists under the utility room will bear the additional weight.

FIFTY-ONE

usiness is brisk in front of a church where parishioners hand out free cases of water from a big, blue and white pyramid. The atmosphere is festive. Balloons wouldn't seem out of place, maybe one of those dancing wind sock characters. I have never been filled with the holy spirit, so far as I can recall, but I envy their joy and exuberance. People mill about on the sidewalk and spill into the street as we ease past in the lumbering ERV.

Coming even with the translucent Mayan temple, a man crows, "Look like y'all need you some water," stretching the final two syllables to breaking—*wah-taah*. He waggles his eyebrows theatrically, peers out over fat, wraparound John Lee Hooker shades. He waits a beat then explodes into knee slapping laughter, mouth yawning and gap-toothed.

I nod, give him a lazy wave, chuckling all the way to the corner. Framed in the side mirror, I see he has resumed business, recalibrated his presence, our moment together drained of color, forgotten.

FIFTY-TWO

President Barack Obama is scheduled to visit Flint today. As it happens, we're both in town at the same time, one man delivering hope to exhausted citizens, the other, warm Alpine Geyser. Flint is wild for the president. Word is, he may pay a visit to Red Cross East Bay Chapter HQ. I fancy crossing paths with him there, or at the cavernous state-run water warehouse out near Bishop airport. Maybe an impromptu photo op on the tiny porch of some incredulous senior citizen, both of us sporting wide grins, shouldering cases of Ice Mountain; POTUS in his blue WH windbreaker, me in my flimsy reflective vest flanked by Secret Service agents, lethally inscrutable behind inkwell shades.

All day long we glimpse evidence of his imminent arrival or recent departure—sudden, heavy State Police presence, barricades, flashing lights, traffic backups, road closures and detours. The grapevine has him turning up on the University of Michigan-Flint campus, a UAW hall, drive-up water distribution site, charter school academy, or any number of churches. Inexplicably, we manage to avoid running into one another. Late in the day, Obama makes a show of waving off bottled water for an ostensible sip of filtered Flint tap in front of a gathering of citizens and press. He meets with Governor Snyder for what's described as a frank and productive discussion; pledges federal assistance. Replacing pipes, the only fix that matters, isn't on the table today.

Heading back to chapter headquarters, empty ERV riding high, clouds threatening rain, I spot Air Force One off in the distance, laboring skyward. The enameled blue-and-white Boeing 747 appears to have been rendered, in one or two quick strokes, onto a moody canvas of gathering storm clouds.

Just a couple of working stiffs at the end of the day, heading home to a shower, maybe a beer before dinner. We gave it all we had, muscles sore, consciences clean. We showed up. Goddamn right, we did.

FIFTY-THREE

I drive slowly up a long, narrow, dead-end parking lot, past a low building divided into cramped studio apartments. Residents sit on stoops and upturned five-gallon buckets, doors propped open to the afternoon heat. The air is heavy, humidity building for a thunderstorm. Turning the ERV around won't be easy, backing out ill-advised. The woman who presumably made the 211 call waves us in. She's heavyset, rising with difficulty from a spindly vinyl dinette chair, her breathing labored. She has a Brita faucet filter new in the box. A nephew promised to install it for her, she informs us. We give her six cases of Aquafina, insurance against the mounting heat.

Neighbors gather, a small crowd begins to form. Available shade is a violet ribbon the length of the building, festooned with white resin chairs, crushed Solo cups, wobbly barbecue grills, smashed foam coolers, empty water bottles, and cockeyed riding toys.

Should I attempt to install her filter? The interior of her unit is dark, impenetrable seen from outside under the flat light of a blazing sun. The ERV blocks vehicle access to the units at the far end of the complex. Her plumbing may or may not accommodate the filter. I have never installed one before; have no idea how to do it properly. Tools may be required. It's probably sweltering inside. Where is an AmeriCorps volunteer when you need one.

Last resort filter pitchers are in short supply, and therefore, very desirable. We always try to keep a few on the truck. I offer one to the woman as a hedge against her no-count nephew— to assuage my guilt. Other women push forward for pitchers of their own. We have many more stops to make. Knots of residents backfill our avenue of retreat. The woman cradles the Brita faucet filter, frets the heat. We run through our supply of water, and most of the replacement filters. I hand out the last two filter pitchers and swing the doors shut. Turning the ERV around is even more difficult than I imagined, in direct proportion to my eagerness to leave. I ease ahead slowly. The gathering parts for us, then reassembles in the shade, birds on a wire awaiting the storm that will soon drive them indoors.

FIFTY-FOUR

lint, a company town famously decimated by a spectacular loss of manufacturing jobs, opportunity and hope, is populated by a majority Black citizenry. Most of means left long ago. Property values have plunged. The tax base, in ruins. Threadbare municipal services presided over by a failed city government and unresponsive state oversight. Driving through town, decades of defeat and hopelessness at every turn, I search for metaphors for the current crisis.

Streets named for dead white poets, Whitman and Emerson, Frost and Bishop, are nothing short of cruel irony. Now and then, my route takes me down Dort Highway for a close-up view of the iconic tower marking the notorious water treatment plant where it all began. FLINT emblazoned in the round, my imagination never failing to add a black skull and crossbones. Like all the other tourists, I take a souvenir snapshot, as good a metaphor as any in a city awash with them.

Crime Scene
Yellow cordon tape hums
low in a stiff breeze
off Saginaw Bay
a norther that scatters
empty evidence markers
the length of Miller Road
Dupont Street alive with eddies
uncapped and droning
Tennyson, Bishop and Frost
lost for words this morning
working my way through
another pallet of water

dead poets urgent
as blue-sky box kite
specks above a crime scene
easing the truck past
houses of the common
abandoned down Whitman
transcendence, surely
for those forbearing souls
over on Emerson.

FIFTY-FIVE

Scores of men, women, and children idle in the vast public spaces of this sprawling warren of Section 8 housing. With school out for summer, few recreation and employment opportunities for Flint youth, and the oppressive languor of a hot July afternoon, what other choice do they have? Residents and visitors are greeted by a cheery welcome sign expressly prohibiting guns and drugs on the premises. A web of narrow streets cross-hatched with speed bumps worthy of Bagram AFB wends through clusters of identical townhouses. The ERV's exhaust system, like the clapper of a great bell, booms off pavement and undercarriage. Carports are located far from front doors, complicating the getting of groceries, small children, and the elderly from car to house. Building numbers and addresses seem concealed from street view by design to some diabolical, unknowable purpose. In practice, it is necessary to wheel water a long way, out of sight of the ERV, in search of individual addresses.

I'm standing in a barren courtyard amid skeletal playground equipment and benches in various states of disrepair, trying to get my bearings. My wife is riding along with me today as an ad hoc Red Cross volunteer. She is anxious to experience firsthand the rewards and challenges of delivering water in Flint. I am grateful for her assistance and her company. I've left her minding the store with instructions to discourage anyone from climbing into the cab or bay of the ERV.

Now, alone in this courtyard among clusters of people who, one can surmise, are living on the brink and nearing the end of their collective rope, I am beginning to have second thoughts. I am able to locate only two of the addresses on my list. I deliver what water I can, and make for the ERV. A small crowd surrounds the vehicle. My wife expresses relief at my return, a sentiment I share. Without fanfare, we suspend official policy of dispensing emergency-only water and supplies. We endeavor to satisfy all comers amid what I would characterize as a carnival atmosphere masking, thinly, an undercurrent of simmering frustration. We emerge from the complex a short time later, bay empty, muffler whanging loudly, bound for the vast water warehouse to reload.

The hi-lo driver swings into action while I stretch out underneath the ERV, wiring up the muffler and tail pipe. The smooth concrete floor, broomed to a low gloss, feels pleasantly cool, offers firm support to a knotty lumbar. Frigates of white clouds ply Delft blue sky, visible through the huge warehouse doors, my wife's firm runners' calves framed in the letterbox space between floor and chassis. Oh, that I could lay here just a little while longer.

FIFTY-SIX

We are dispatched to work off hot sheets or follow well-established routes. I never manage to finish all the addresses I'm given, a thick sheaf of paper on a clipboard. The city is divided into operational zones. An efficient route system has been established. Teams work their way through neighborhoods methodically, street by street, unless they're hopscotching the city working 211 calls. Maybe it's the weather, or chemistry between team members, but some days are imbued with an adrenal sense of urgency, other's laconic as a day gig delivering the Yellow Pages—back when people still did that sort of thing. This is one of those days.

They are sitting on nylon camp chairs in the driveway, facing the street, cluttered garage open behind them. It's a pristine Michigan summer day, blue sky stretched tight over the springy green armature of a July afternoon. Stalin and Churchill hale and hearty, side by side at Yalta minus a dying FDR, his ghost image haunting the space between them. I've forgotten their names, a pair of old men just passing time, biggest battles behind them, something cool to drink in Solo cups on a small round, plastic table. They make child care look easy. Even inviting. They're watching the grandkids—one of them is, anyway. The other is here for moral support. They seem genuinely happy to see us, broad smiles glimpsed from the street, still radiating as we approach. Theirs must be the only chairs available. Otherwise, I'm certain we would have been offered our own. They have pro forma questions about the water delivery business, where we're from, the features of the ERV.

They chuckle a great deal and fill the not-uncomfortable conversational gaps with rote comfort food like "yessir" and "that's it, that's it" and "there you go, there you go" and "you right about that."

We cover the Tigers, lack of rain, traffic, the state of Michigan roads, the pathos of the Lions, and touch on general health issues, nothing too personal. No one mentions the political machinations underlying our presence, or the elephant in the room: institutional racism and all its discontents. To this day, I can't say for certain we even left them any water. I wish I would have asked permission to take their picture. A portrait of old friends, arrived at the crest of the present on the wave of the past, thin-lipped line of sea and sky mum on any hint of the future.

FIFTY-SEVEN

The Pulitzer Prize-winning novelist Richard Ford, a Michigan State University alumnus, taught public school at Flint's Whittier Junior High in the early sixties. In one of his Frank Bascombe novels, Ford has his Everyman, New Jersey realtor, reflect wistfully on a visit he and his wife once paid to Flint for a spur-of-the-moment, larky look-see.

A few years ago, Ford and his wife made their own pilgrimage to Flint, drawn by fond memories of having lived and worked there at the zenith of its prosperity. With General Motors paying the freight, schools, libraries, parks, streets, and hospitals were top notch back then—downtown vibrant and alive. The Fords discovered Whittier Junior High abandoned, about to be razed, in their estimation. They were unable to locate their old neighborhood—never mind the house where they had once happily resided on Miller Road.

Harmless fun to imagine bumping into old Frank coming out of a Dunkin' Donuts on Dupont Avenue in his barracuda jacket, fob to the big Crown Vic spinning on his finger. We'd exchange pleasantries; talk baseball and Emerson and life in Haddam. Bascombe, a longtime volunteer *Sponsor*—a Samaritan with time on his hands willing to listen and offer free, friendly, practical advice to a fellow citizen—could be counted on for discretion and sound guidance. I'd offer him a bottle of Poland Spring and we'd part ways, both of us a little lighter for the chance encounter.

FIFTY-EIGHT

Disaster is officially declared in Flint. It is 2015, well over a year since unsuspecting residents were first exposed to toxic levels of lead and biohazardous effluence. Tractor trailers full of donated bottled water arrive daily from points north, south, east, and west. Flint is world news, a symbol of the fraying fabric of American civic responsibility and the nation's decaying infrastructure. Even Cher dispatches a semi or two. Residents are urged not to drink or bathe in unfiltered tap. The state provides filters for standard kitchen faucets, but not for tub or shower fixtures. Rumors abound that shower filters are available to the well-connected. Physicians treat patients for lead toxicity, rashes, and Legionella bacterial infection. Water for drinking, cooking, and bathing; for pets, medical care, teeth-brushing, and ice, comes in sixteen-ounce bottles that end up filling thousands of recycling bags or accumulating in great glittering heaps in backyards and vacant lots.

I hear the reports, make a mental note to investigate further, but fail to register the magnitude of the disaster. Truth is, I'm barely listening. We've planned a family reunion in Tennessee to celebrate Ima Nell's upcoming birthday. She's survived surgery, most of her small intestine removed, wheelchair-bound, alive but greatly diminished. She's living in a nursing home three miles equidistant from the small farm where she grew up and her old condo. My brother and I have spent months driving back and forth arranging for her care, battling bureaucracy, tracking the decaying orbit of her life. She steadfastly refuses to rejoin us in Michigan. She seems to be losing her grip on reality, but outwardly, remains optimistic and accepting of her circumstances.

We haul in pizza, ice cream, and cake, enough for twenty. But it's Saturday—only a weekend skeleton crew on duty, essential personnel only. A couple of aides and a harried nurse wander through the common room. They politely decline cake, eye the pizza non-committedly. Group pictures are taken. Old jokes rehashed. Ribbing of the good-natured variety flows. We box lots of leftovers, stash everything in the staff refrigerator, all of us due to fly out the following day.

"Happy birthday to you. Happy birthday to you. Happy birthday dear mother. Happy birthday to you." She'll be dead in a few weeks, one day shy of her eighty-third birthday.

FIFTY-NINE

Flint is among the most dangerous cities in the United States. It has a murder rate to rival that of Detroit and St. Louis. The public schools are abysmal. For-profit charter schools proliferate for the financial benefit of wealthy investors such as Betsy DeVos, current Secretary of Education, conservative ideologues from the west side of the state, and the Lansing politicians who rely on their financial support. Youth unemployment soars. Median family income, low and dropping. A city beset with gang violence, a rampant drug trade, and broken families.

Generational hopelessness and institutional racism, like tainted water, touch everyone. Pestilence, harkening back to the Old Testament. If it's retribution you're after, what was the offense?

Cue the locusts, cue the rain of frogs.

SIXTY

A woman living on a street slowly reverting to woodland greets us with a smile. Windows minus screens, thrown open to a gorgeous summer day, doors banging in the breeze on their hinges. I note the robins' nest tucked into a corner of the rickety porch awning. She says baby birds are visible from the front door. I heard them keening on the way in. The smell inside is overpowering, water supply shut off who knows how long ago. Empty pet food cans, water bowls, chew toys, scratching posts, scattered newspapers, plastic crates, and nesting blankets abound, evidence we are in the presence of a dedicated animal lover. Dogs bark nonstop from the other side of a closed door. Cats slink in from outside, then slink back out again. It wouldn't surprise me to discover nesting squirrels in the dishwasher or a family of raccoons hunkered in the tub. Soon, the young birds will vacate the nest, fleeing this place, never to return.

SIXTY-ONE

A grand old pile sweeps into view, all swinging gutters, curling shingles, and peeling portico. The side door is open behind steel crime bars. I rap on the heavy metal frame, announce myself. A chair scrapes in the gloom, the floor groans. An unpleasant cooking smell wafts through the bars. A very large man with a shaved head appears at the top of the stairs. I can't see his face clearly in the shadows. He is eating something soft the color of spray foam insulation, excess clinging to his cheek and lip. Shirtless, he's wearing baggy shorts, flip-flops, and a huge silver sidearm holstered heavy on his hip. Without a word he gestures to leave the water on the driveway near the door. I consider asking if the gun is loaded, but manage to stop myself just in time.

SIXTY-TWO

I take an instant dislike to Gail. Spare, compact, she has a way of speaking that's all business: I brought my own teabag, thank you very much. Not a nickel more. At ease, soldier, smoke 'em if you got 'em.

In fact, Gail is a retired United States Army nurse of respectable rank, a woman of a certain age, a flinty slip of a gal. Her late husband, a career military man, a Vietnam vet. They were stationed in all the predictable places—Florida, California, Virginia, Hawaii, Texas. I imagine the type of nurse who would judge me harshly for my urine output, browbeat me into holding off on my next Vicodin, shrink me down to size with a curt "seen one, ya seen 'em all." I'm relieved when our day together draws to an end. Not because Gail hasn't shouldered her share of the burden, or been particularly unpleasant. First impressions are like prime parking spaces— hard to give up. I hang on to mine like a dog on a bone.

Gail and I will be paired on several different occasions during my time in Flint. It only occurs to me later that she would not have allowed herself to be paired a second time with someone who irritated her in the slightest. Unlike me, Gail would fold her arms, fix the relevant authority with a steely gaze, prepared to go to the mat. Little by little, I discover Gail possesses a wry sense of humor. I don't mind so much when she criticizes my driving. She takes particular glee when I run the ERV up over curbs, points it out with relish, screens her mouth with her hand like she's confiding a secret to remind me we're rolling on dually wheels. I picture the two of us barreling down some Levantine desert track in a bullet-pocked Humvee, Gail attuned to every suspicious mound, cardboard box, and rock pile, barking "get your head out of your ass, soldier!" When I box us in on cul-de-sacs or impassible one-way streets, she leaps out, jogs fifty yards behind the ERV and directs me backing up with complicated hand gestures that wouldn't look out of place on a carrier deck. This isn't her first time at bat. She saw duty in New York City following Hurricane Sandy, served in New Orleans in the aftermath of Katrina.

She bunks with the AmeriCorps kids in their downtown Flint dorm. Home is mid-Michigan or Colorado, I can't remember which. She flies back and forth to see her grandkids. The AmeriCorps kids hang together after-hours and on days off. Gail keeps to herself, eats off a hot plate, sleeps poorly, and is losing weight she can ill afford. The dorm rooms are hot and stuffy. Wi-Fi is harder to find than a Kirtland's warble. When we're gathered as a group in the Red Cross volunteer muster room, Gail can often be heard bitching, sotto voce, about policies and procedures, the bureaucracy—but down the chain of command, never up. Little by little, I come to understand she has suffered loss aplenty. *Underneath that gruff exterior*, as they say. We don't establish anything close to friendship, but perhaps, with time, we would have.

I tend to err on the side of self-deprecation—own beachfront there. Gail is on to me, but doesn't take advantage. She has grit in abundance, which I find appealing. Armor enough to remind me life is an indiscriminate and unforgiving flinger of slings and arrows. Good luck, all you artful dodgers and the flak-jacketed. You can look for me among the pin-cushioned, quilled with fletching. Gail would find this amusing.

SIXTY-THREE

All morning long we weave a crazy web in this forgotten corner of the city near Max Brandon Park. The street we are on does not invite the soul to linger. This particular house, though consumptive in appearance like all the rest, is distinguished by neat red and white trim. Coke signs hang in the windows. There's one posted near the front door next to a note written in a careful hand—Please Go To Back Door. No sign of a dog, but here's another Coke sign in the back window. I knock repeatedly, no answer, so I beat it back to the ERV. Coming even with the corner of the house, I spot a low-slung sedan as it sweeps into view. It careens into the driveway, windows opaque, deep bass pulsating, keeping rhythm with my hammering heart. My reflective disaster relief vest suddenly feels gossamer thin, like a cheap Halloween costume—one of the lesser superheroes. The driver's door swings open, revealing four glowering young men. The driver steps out.

"Red Cross water," I offer—repeat as protective mantra.

It's his mother's house. She's not home, but needs eight cases and Brita replacement cartridges. Inside, it's dim, curtains drawn, air still and close, silence a disinterested third party. Coca-Cola memorabilia hangs everywhere. Walls painted red and white. There's a big illuminated Coke clock on the wall in the tiny kitchen. Classic Coke rug.

The young man grins and shakes his head. "She's crazy for the stuff." Turns out she grew up in Atlanta. Worked at corporate. I don't ask in what capacity, but I'm betting she didn't occupy a corner office.

We stand in silence for few moments, taking it all in, me for the first time, the young man, perhaps, nursing a familiar ambivalence. How to reconcile a conflicted Southern heritage, an old woman's pride, and deep abiding love. I envy him, this thoughtful young man who I had so badly misjudged only moments before. Someone a mother could be proud of.

SIXTY-FOUR

The Flint River was widely known to be polluted years before the city, under state control, decided to leave the costly Detroit water system. As soon as untreated river water resumed flowing through aging pipes, it bit into the soft metal and lead levels spiked at the tap. General Motors, still operating one or two plants in town, had long since switched from the river as an industrial water source to prevent metal corrosion and protect its bottom line. Driving past vast weedy concrete prairie of demolished factories, I'm reminded of the quote by the late Charles Wilson, former General Motors CEO: "I thought what was good for our country was good for General Motors, and vice versa." Wilson's statement, often misquoted, proved prescient, at least in respect to safe, reliable water.

SIXTY-FIVE

The Kearsley Park neighborhood feels pastoral on a warm, spring day. Large swaths of verdant, vacant land thrive where houses, garages, gardens, and porches once stood. A riot of weeds, tangle of vines, saplings, and thorn bushes swallow busted apron, old sycamore, and blackened foundation, all of it overlaid with littered, glittering street grid. Arm out the window, I take in the sun-dappled, sweet-smelling morning. I imagine thriving populations of deer, fox, coyote, lynx, wild turkey, and hawks. Squinting transforms the landscape to soft-focus savanna, a geography favored by our ancestors fresh from the trees, affording long, early-warning vistas.

Same place one week later; the day an overcast and oppressively hot one. I'm stricken by an undeniable sense of unease and foreboding. The lack of contrasting light and shadow flattens the scenery. The air is still as a corpse. Nothing stirs, but the landscape and all it contains seems resigned to an imminent, great gust of wind. The undergrowth feels pregnant with unseen danger. Abandoned houses are nothing less than great blackened lungs gasping for breath, cellars flooded, standing black water gleaming with oil sheen, hollow shells harboring the unsettled ghosts of America's once proud middle class.

SIXTY-SIX

I recall being in Flint on only three occasions before deploying with Red Cross Disaster Relief. Twenty-five years ago, we attended a Jeff Daniels concert at the Whiting Auditorium. I recall his sweet, wistful version of the Civil War ballad "Michigan, My Michigan." A few years later, I watched my wife finish the Crim Festival of Races half-marathon run through rolling hills and leafy streets of some of the city's nicer neighborhoods. Flint turned out in numbers to cheer the runners on and offer cooling mists from garden hoses. My first visit was forty-some years ago to attend a backyard barbecue. I cruised in past the mammoth Buick City complex, sporting pastel clam diggers cinched with a jaunty nautical rope belt. I got drunk as a lord in my jackass pants, then drove home looking like a harlequin sketched by Jules Feiffer.

Flint, when I thought about the city at all, was an unfortunate municipal abstraction a few exits south of the faux-gemütlich hokum of Frankenmuth, Frostian fork in the road where heavy southbound traffic on I-75 is relieved by the US-23 split, siphoning cars off to Ann Arbor, easing my drive home from many an idyllic northern vacation. It pains me to admit I'd never even bothered to pull off for a Halo Burger, chili fries, and a shake.

SIXTY-SEVEN

The Speedway on MLK is unusually crowded for a weekday morning. Surrounding the pump island, a gridlock of cars and a wrecker having just deposited a beat-up blue sedan. Despite steady rain, all the vehicles' occupants are milling around in tense tableaux, glaring and gesturing at one another. I'm behind the wheel of the ERV, watching from across the intersection, waiting for the light to change. The wipers keep time to a song on a country station favored by my partner. I prefer silence, but I eat my peanut butter and jelly sandwich in quiet forbearance.

The light turns green, and the scrum across the street jells suddenly, organizing itself into opposing teams of shouting combatants, everyone brandishing pepper spray, arms extended, free hands covering faces in a futile attempt to deflect the noxious agent. The ERV leads a stalled parade of cars waiting to proceed into the intersection, but no one moves because I'm not about to steer us into a street brawl and the possibility of gunplay. Suddenly, the battle of the gas pumps ends in a draw, everyone leaping into vehicles and speeding away, presumably weeping and trailing gouts of snot. It's over in thirty seconds.

The light goes from yellow to red. I take another bite and turn my face to the rain through the open window while Dierks Bentley yodels a tune. Something about being drunk on a plane.

SIXTY-EIGHT

In 2013, then-Governor Rick Snyder, numbers guy by trade and inclination, appoints Darnell Early Flint's third consecutive emergency manager. A Republican-dominated legislature passed PA-436 the previous year, allowing the governor to install his proxy, usurping the authority of elected representatives in financially distressed municipalities and school districts, in exchange for state financial assistance. The law was crafted to prevent voter interference. Early, charged with slashing spending, signs off on tapping the river without properly treating the water.

Six years later, the criminal prosecutions of Early and other state and city officials responsible for poisoning the citizens of Flint remain unresolved. Snyder left office due to term limits. Bill Schutte, attorney general during the crisis and critic of Snyder, soundly lost his bid for Snyder's old seat. The new attorney general threw out Schutte's woefully inept investigation, and vowed to open a new one. Snyder was recently named as a defendant in a class-action lawsuit brought by the victims. Harvard withdrew a teaching offer. A judge ordered the surrender of his cell phone and other electronic devices.

The city of Flint struggles to replace old lead water lines, and children born at the beginning of the crisis, or shortly before, come of school age. Dr. Mona Hanna-Attisha, the pediatrician who first alerted the world to the impending health disaster, wrote a book about the magnitude of the suffering visited on her patients and the community. During the summer of 2019, the citizens of Newark, New Jersey are advised not to drink their tap water, and are furnished with bottled. The chemical PFAS threatens the groundwater of many Michigan communities situated near old military bases, affecting a cross section of people of different races, cultures, socioeconomic levels, sexual preferences, and gender identities. Environmental crises are efficient equalizers. The water supply of the city of Ann Arbor, home to the University of Michigan, is threatened by an underground plume of chemicals leached from an old manufacturing plant in town. Go, Wolverines! Go, while you still can.

My parents raised us in a time of postwar plenty for the privileged white majority. We learned to live with the prospect of nuclear annihilation, mankind's quaint existential quandary at the time, and took no notice of the slowly metastasizing cancer eating away at the nation's core—climate change, institutional racism, partisan rancor, authoritarianism, unchecked corporate power in the form of unlimited campaign contributions and economic inequality.

The cure, if there is one, may be sufficiently drastic as to test the resilience of the American proposition, or forever disabuse us of the myth of American exceptionalism. In the meantime, a novel virus has spontaneously broken out of Wuhan, China and spread worldwide. It's busy rearranging the furniture in humankind's den in ways no one can yet predict.

SIXTY-NINE

Flynn grew up in Flint in the early eighties. "Things way better now than they was back then. Lots of shootin', drugs, 'n gangs," he says.

Flynn is new to the job, hired by the state to service the endless water needs of Flint residents. He rides along with me today, holding forth, an easygoing man of good humor and grace. Governor Snyder prides himself on his prowess as a free market job creator. Flynn lost a decent private sector job the year previous, but thanks to the governor's new public sector jobs initiative, he earns eleven dollars an hour delivering water to those lacking the means to get it for themselves. Flynn lives in a neighborhood beset by violence. He won't allow his twelve-year-old son to play outdoors, so the boy will spend a good deal of his summer vacation indoors playing video games. Flynn credits the neighborhood gang members of his youth for steering him away from serious trouble. He gives me a daylong tutorial on the balance of power in various neighborhoods, places I have driven through many times, blissfully ignorant of the politics churning just below the surface. Turf war served hot and cold. Economic desperation, the cultural common dominator, trumps race in the poorest neighborhoods.

Pop, pop, pop. We sit at a stop light on the eve of the long Independence Day weekend. "Fireworks," I ask?

"Nine-millimeter," says Flynn. Earlier this morning, we stood transfixed at the back of the ERV as a car whipped around the corner and fishtailed into a nearby driveway. An agitated-looking woman bolted the vehicle, hand in the waistband of her stretch pants. Flynn insisted we leave at once.

He confides he has a concealed handgun permit. I assume he is carrying. Despite myself, I feel safer by magnitudes, compounding the shame of having felt relief when Flynn and I were paired together this morning. A Black sidekick to validate my privileged white liberal cred. An armed and savvy local. How lucky can an already lucky guy get? Will my self-satisfied sense of racial equanimity and anti-gun sentiment still take my calls after today?

Flynn likes guns. He's a proud NRA member, ticks off an owner's list of long guns and handguns. Speaks rapturously of ammo specs, muzzle velocity, and stopping power. "I want me an AK," Flynn says.

I bite. "The fuck you want with a Kalashnikov?"

Flynn yammers on about reliability, magazine capacity, ease of operation. Then he grins broadly, casts a sly, sideways glance. "Man, didn't you used to love them *Die Hard* movies?"

"Bruce Willis made AK's sexy, is that it?" We talk easily, laugh like hyenas, part ways like beet-faced Shriners at days end. Where did the time go?

SEVENTY

My partner mentions in passing the significance of today's date. We make small talk, the work day only just beginning. It's *4/20*, just another social meme, one of thousands rushing past in a torrent every day. I'm familiar with the term. Hal is fishing for my views on pot, medicinal or otherwise. He hints that he is considering observing the erstwhile holiday when the work day is done, and is curious to know my opinion. I have none; at least, none I'm willing to share with Hal.

Mid-morning, we park in front of a small bungalow, front porch a hive of activity. Young women herd small children toward a beat-up sedan idling in the driveway. We've interrupted the early stages of a what looks to be a long, unhurried house party in the cramped living room. Six young men ring a low coffee table. A pall of smoke blankets the room. It smells of skunk and sweet confectionary dreams. There's a tense moment triggered by the open question of our identities and intentions, but once bona fides are established, everyone relaxes and festivities resume.

We're directed to stack ten cases of Dasani in the kitchen, leaving no choice but to repeatedly thread a narrow path through the middle of the party. On my last trip through, I'm invited, disingenuously I assume, to join the fun. I try to imagine the dramatic shift in mood were I to accept; shoehorn myself onto the ecru microfiber sectional and rub my palms together in gleeful anticipation, like George Hanson, the Jack Nicholson character in *Easy Rider*. Moments later we're on our way to the next stop, vanished—up in smoke.

SEVENTY-ONE

It's my first day ride-along, yet I find myself behind the wheel of the big yellow Penske box truck. The woman training me informs me she is on her seventy-second consecutive day of deployment in Flint. Christine prefers not to drive the truck. She drove us from chapter headquarters to the vehicle marshalling yard in her beat-up Focus first thing this morning. The memory of that harrowing ride still fresh, I am more than happy to take the wheel. Winter, a long, gray, cold one, she recounts icy stairs, sopping feet, and snow-covered walkways. National Guard escorts. Heavy State Police presence. It's snowing big wet flakes, spring still weeks away. In the rear, two pallets of bottled water ride upended like old seabed thrust up by plate tectonics, heaped atop the wheel wells. I dumped them turning too sharply out of the warehouse lot onto Carpenter Road.

"My God, look at that place," I say, jabbing a thumb toward a forlorn mobile home park. A shifting landscape of colorless trailers hunker among black, skeletal trees, branches utterly convincing as the fingers of a lost race of spectral giants.

Christine doesn't suffer fools. "Ain't bad compared to some. My aunt used to live there."

Hours later we're headed back to the warehouse, cold, tired, and wet. It's snowing fine dust, sunset bullied into submission by shouldering clouds. "Now, this one is really bad," Christine says, looking out the window.

A low place, scrub woods, dark forms dissolving into twilight. The trailers nearest the road look like gaping skulls, black holes once fitted with windows and doors. Aluminum long since stripped, insulation exposed, they appear in twilight as dirty bales of cotton randomly scattered across the landscape. Oncoming night, damp, encroaching woods have rubbed away what's left of the place. Christine says there are squatters.

I peer into the gloom, looking for cooking fires. Oncoming headlights illuminate the road ahead—torches of the king's men bearing news of plague, braving a shortcut, black woods closing in from all sides. My collar and shoes are soaked. I'm shivering from cold—the cold and nothing more.

SEVENTY-TWO

I visit the cemetery the afternoon following her death. The funeral director suggested I inspect the plot to avoid any surprises. She had arranged a cozy interment next to her beloved parents in a small country cemetery situated next to a lovely old, white clapboard United Methodist Church, known locally as Eden. Chapel and cemetery sit across the road from a tidy farm once owned by my maternal great-grandfather. I am told this by Ray, the sextant, after a frustrating search for her flush marker ahead of the arrival of the backhoe guy. Record keeping, Ray demurs, is practiced casually in these parts. I'd no sooner mentioned the family name, Nave, than Ray fills in the missing pieces for me. I recall hearing how the Naves were forced to leave the area in the 30s when the Tennessee Valley Authority claimed the land through eminent domain and transformed it to a reservoir behind the Douglas Dam.

Ray owns the farm. He asks whether I might know of any previous internments below the flat stone inscribed with her name and date of birth. Momentarily speechless, I reply that, absent accurate records, I can think of only one way to find out with any certainty. We bury her two days later in her own few cubic feet of red Tennessee clay, the day fine and warm.

With the approach of the first anniversary of my mother's death, I am gripped by an urge to visit her grave. The day is much like that sorrowful first one, sunny and warm, hint of autumn in the trees. I place a small wreath of flowers, stand in awkward silence, will myself into a properly somber state, invoke the spirit of some culminating truth. But I feel only the heat of the day, hear the drone of insects, lobes of distant trees swaying in the breeze, the overall effect a not-unpleasant torpor. Four years on, I am no longer drawn to Eden. She is gone and I am here, at large in the world, beyond hope of redemption bestowed by another, a man working hard to regain himself, alive to the presence of an old, deep abiding love, waiting, hovering just outside my awareness.

SEVENTY-THREE

I take everything in at a glance—sink, television, low hills of upholstery rising above stacks of newspapers and bulging garbage bags. A grimy stove and fridge, opaque windows, and an antique rollaway bed. Irregular shapes in the middle-distance breach against dim walls, and recede into gloom. We stack water wherever we can. My partner notes the red indicator on the faucet filter. The man, seated in a wide manual wheelchair with no footrests, wears a shapeless red pocket T over a great expanse of belly. His faded, sackcloth sweat pants, also red. His long hair, the color of old piano ivory, beard patchy and white. Toenails, like flakes of shale from a sluice pan. He looks by turns startled and agitated.

I study framed black-and-white photos carefully arranged on the wall. Vintage Pershing tank, officers in khaki and white dress belts; a smiling handshake medal tableau. There sits an enormous canvasback truck on white sand, a flotilla of puffy white clouds, palm trees, and a guard tower right out of a World War II war movie. "What branch were you in?" I ask.

One eye floats adrift, a battered blueberry bobbing in buttermilk. Right hand, contracted like a broken wing, two fingers missing. "That's my old man. Marines. My boy, too. Twenty years." He sits up straighter, narrows his clear eye.

Jarheads, the three of them. His war, Vietnam. One tour. 1967. He goes quiet again, slumps in his chair, addresses the floor. "Was a hunert' and forty-nine of us went over. They's only four come back." A long, deafening silence follows.

"Were you at Khe Sanh?" I ask.

More silence. Then, an emphatic "yes."

Perhaps he really did survive the hell of that infamous ridgetop, or some other forgotten piece of Highland real estate. Distinctions seem superfluous. A United States Marine, I have no doubt he's a lifetime member of Hell's loyalty program. On the porch sits a small lidless wooden box full of straw. I puzzled over it on the way in. I glance again on my way out. Too small, even for a lap dog. Just right for a plastic baby Jesus.

Besieged on high
Old St. Nick hums
Silent Night soft and low
to ward off the deafening din
of the rising waters below.

SEVENTY-FOUR

Throughout spring and summer 2015, I field a steady stream of calls from the nursing home. April, Shel, Ashley, or Karen the Wound-Care-Nurse, calling with updates, alerts, and prognostications. The pace picks up as summer wanes:

cut her leg fell out of bed can't won't eat ate won't can't get out bed fell chair bed bruised dehydrated motivated expiated aspirated sweet thing sweet Jesus sweet hereafter well swell swelling swollen weep skin paper thin tight as a drum breakdown PT OT RN MD RA CHF ER UTI VA PA DNR OMG WTF pressure sore ulceration toe backside heel hip more Lasix less Coumadin more or less is more less than never-the-less never complains never gives up never ever asleep awake beauty shop day trip coney dogs pine cone doll memory book doctor took a look progress plateaued upswing downturn rebound tests more tests transfusion confusion contusion delusion night and day and day and night and night sweats night nurse transfixed transferred arm leg heel bottom thin skin swollen swelling ballooned breakdown downward ulcer skin weeping wavering waffling weep for me for her weep through wraps sweet thing sweet as pie sweet Jesus sweet by-and-by goodbye good luck good God call back bruise cut bandage wrap call back later blood loss find sweet Jesus find a way two pints to weep find a way so sweet will I find church choir Elvis Tuesday oldies games shows

Ellen sing-a-long a way to say will I find a way will
I better worse no trouble at all delight asleep awake
no matter of time short staffed two person transfer
belt find a way to weep will I find sign off tests
confused two more pints rash temp cough low blood
count admitted more tests transfuse inconclusive
confusement two units vitals good come can you
don't can you don't come come can you should I
don't come maybe time to come yes time it's time
time yes its time now is the time the time is now—

A kind of jazz, I learn to listen for music in the spaces
between the notes of their words.

SEVENTY-FIVE

AQUAhydrate, a California bottling company marketing high-end designer water, generously donates their product to Flint residents. Sean "P Diddy" Combs and Mark Walhberg are investors in, and promoters of, the brand. The water is known here as *Diddy Water*. I'm told that on days when AQUAhydrate is available at neighborhood distribution centers, demand quickly outpaces supply, ratcheting up tension between residents and water volunteers. Diddy Water is a valuable underground commodity with strong social media legs. News travels fast. A casual black market prevails.

What distinguishes AQUAhydrate from Flint tap is the punchline to a bad joke—from the brands of its competitors, is anyone's guess. I deliver Dasani and Mountain Valley, Ice Mountain and Poland Spring, but in five months of deployment, I never lay eyes on a bottle of Diddy Water, and come to think of it as urban legend.

SEVENTY-SIX

An elderly man stands on his porch, reed thin but for the small planet of his belly beneath a Lynyrd Skynyrd, "Gimme Back My Bullets" tank. Lank gray ponytail, dry as sisal twine. He says he needs eight cases of *whateveryougot* and some Pur filter cartridges. Had his water tested last month, "got a real good reading." Gem of a morning, we agree, things heating up this afternoon, for sure.

"My buddy's coming over with his Fender." They still get together to jam.

"Play in any bands?" I ask.

"Lots of 'em, dude." Wants to know if I've ever heard of Black Powder. Drop Forge. "How about Blues Regents?"

I shake my head, opting for the truth. I hope I haven't disappointed him too much. He probably went to junior high with the guys from Grand Funk Railroad, local sons who made it big. Maybe he worked as a roadie for Terry Knight and the Pack for beer and entrée to hippie chicks from Central Michigan University, but I think better of asking. Pulling away from the curb, accelerating past dilapidated houses sandwiched between overgrown vacant lots, I wonder who's left to complain about the noise, the ultimate validation for any self-respecting garage band.

SEVENTY-SEVEN

"I like suckers." A simple declaration I try and fail to understand in the silence that follows. I don't interpret it as a request, which it certainly is. Part of the problem, the boy speaking has the softest voice, one that's nearly inaudible to me. He is seven, maybe eight. The other element contributing to our impasse is the State Police cruiser three doors down, red lights blazing, the first moments of a traffic stop in progress.

He's one of a trio sitting on a low block wall in front of the house next door to the one we've been searching for. Neighbors on porches escaping the heat observe the drama unfolding between the trooper and the occupant of the suspect vehicle. My partner, a retired nurse, stands on the front porch, hands open, palms out, signaling for ten cases. We dispatch our duty quickly and efficiently. The boys, faces alive with equal measure sweetness and mischief, like the stitched covers of spinning baseballs, follow our progress from the ERV to the house and back. Here it comes again, a bit louder—*I like suckers*—only this time it's directed to my partner.

"Oh, my goodness, I'm just so sorry sweetheart, I haven't got a sucker for you today. I sure wish I did, though." Even I heard him clearly this time. I detect a flicker in his eyes. A reflection of the patrol car's flashing lights, or something else?

Carefully, I pull away from the curb, ease the ERV around the tableaux of trouble just ahead. All four doors open wide, the sweating trooper, beefy hands encased in gelatin-green surgical gloves, rifles the contents of the glove compartment. The driver, a thin sallow woman, stands handcuffed in front of the car. She levels a hateful glare as we pass.

Suckers—colorful nuggets done up in cellophane twists; an enduring, simple pleasure. Moments a patient child can extend into sweet eternity.

SEVENTY-EIGHT

backhoe excavates a piebald front yard on a block of aluminum-sided bungalows. Half the houses on this street are empty and abandoned. The man we're speaking with wears a pensive expression. We watch the dark pit in his neighbor's front yard deepen. He takes a deep drag from a cigarette and shakes his head in disgust. "The fuckin' city should just give the abandoned houses to all them homeless vets."

He wears his frizzy silver hair tied back in a bushy horse's mane, eyes moist and owlish behind huge lenses. "Did you serve?" I ask, presuming a stint with the Rangers in the Delta or perhaps a tour with the MPs at Tan Son Nhat.

He looks at me, incredulous, as if I've accused him of composing sonnets in a Romance language or harboring a secret obsession with *Mamma Mia*. "Fuck no!" doubling over with laughter, contrails of blue smoke jetting from his nostrils.

With a rending metallic squeal, the backhoe yanks a jagged graph line of infamous pipe from the reluctant earth. Up the street, contractors pour new sidewalks. This neighborhood appears to be getting a new lease on life. Randomness reigns. Some make do with a Band-Aid, while others seem doomed to die waiting for an organ donor.

SEVENTY-NINE

Consider, for a moment, the front doors of Flint. With a brisk knock or press of a button, admittance gained or denied. Access is often obstructed; a pit bull chained to a porch or pacing unchained in a driveway, stairs too rotten to bear weight or no stairs at all, a barrier of overgrown yews. A surprising number of houses have functioning doorbells and discrete high-tech security cameras. Steel crime bars resonate poorly when rapped with the knuckles. Signage is common, homemade and commercial—Beware of Dog. Use Side Door–Back Door. No Trespassing. No Solicitors. No Parking. Biker Lives Here.

Jesus savesliveslovesforgiveswatchesoveryouiscomingdiedforyoursins. Shoot 'Em All—Let God Sort the Bodies. Neighborhood Watch. Area Under Surveillance. Bill and Helen Van Cortland. The Samuelson's. Security By Smith and Wesson. Beware Pit Doberman, German Shephard, Rottweiler. For Rent. For Lease. For Sale. Price Reduced. Best Offer. Condemned. Keep Out. Pet's Inside. Oxygen In Use.

Symbols and logos abound—Stars and stripes. Stars and bars. Blue Stars. Gold Stars. Crucifixes. Jack Daniels. Cannabis leaves. Genesee County Sheriff's Association. UAW. NRA. AFSME. ACLU. Highwaymen. Outlaws. Harley-Davidson. No Dumping. Colt. Colt 45. Hennessy. Smith and Wesson. Unicorns. Angels. AR 15's. Cobra Gunships. Bud Light. Flapping Christmas decorations. Vivint. Brinks. ADT—the rare realtor's sign.

Planters on rusty hooks, wind chimes, sun catchers, and welcome mats. Flags snap on yard poles or from wall sconces—American, Confederate, Jolly Roger, Union Jack,

Christian, U of M, Michigan State, Central, Western, Ferris.

Porches of every description—cracked slab concrete, buckled tongue and groove, warped decking or delaminated plywood covered in powdery Astroturf or old paint, original color visible at the margins. Covered or uncovered, screened or open-air. Many of them list and sag, support wobbly railing draped with stiff gray throw rugs, top rail patterned with cigarette burns, spattered with bird shit. Stairs pitch toward streets, treads broken or missing. Ramps are common; aluminum skeleton topped with dirt shedding plate, most of them nothing more than angular abstract sculpture cobbled from treated two-by and half-inch ply.

Porches are purgatory for household debris destined for the curb—toys, apparel, broken appliances, packaging, wet carpet, fast food wrappers, disintegrating cardboard boxes, mops, pails, swollen bricks of disposable diapers, food scraps, pet food cans, plastic milk crates, packing peanuts, returnable bottles and, of course, empty water bottles in bags, bins, or rolling willy-nilly in the breeze. Everything mingling with rusting barbecue grills, webbed patio chairs, plastic tables, cases of water stacked ten high, pet crates, and sand-filled coffee cans spiked with cigarette butts. Side entrances are, by contrast, Spartan affairs, utilitarian in aspect. The front door draws like a magnet, portal to interior worlds I feel humbled to enter.

EIGHTY

Reloading, relaxing outside the ERV parked inside the vast oasis of the state-leased water warehouse located in an industrial park adjacent to Bishop Airport. Armed corrections officers loom large in black, quasi-military kit; skinny, orange-jumpsuited felons waltz dust mops wide as the wingspan of a Beechcraft. The press reports that water donations are slowing. The State of Michigan makes up the difference, bears more and more of the cost of purchasing water wholesale and furnishing it to Flint residents. The city turns up less and less in the daily news cycle; newer, more compelling stories supplanting the novelty of a domestic water crisis. What had, in the beginning, felt like a dire mission of mercy at full boil, Berlin Airlift writ small, has been dialed back to a simmer in the public eye.

Disaster relief has become routine and reliable in a long, desultory siege. An entire bottled water bureaucracy and infrastructure has sprung up in place of the invisible, efficient, unsung network of pipes everyone took for granted. Is *Disaster Relief Operation* still an accurate description? Red Cross resources are finite; other competing regional, state, and national disasters, surely on the horizon. Word is, taxpayers will assume full responsibility for providing water to Flint residents before summers end. Administration spokespeople in Lansing are already floating trial balloons, claiming that lead levels are dropping to normal limits. No one I speak with expresses trust in anything coming from the capital or city hall.

Culpability, despite all the finger pointing out of Lansing, is hardly in doubt. Where to send the final bill, however, remains an open question. I follow the progress of the hi-lo operator, billed cap and fork tower floating disembodied in the distance, gliding over a placid, glittering blue and white sea. If he arrives with a pallet of Diddy Water, I silently vow to block the bay of the ERV and ask him to bring a less notorious brand. Water, like oxygen, is an elemental part of human existence, our bodies humming in endless exchange. I want to pretend, if only for a moment, it remains the purest of elements, sweet, crisp, and refreshing. Free of lead, biological agents, mercury, arsenic, benzene, celebrity, and political calculation. A human right, something all are entitled to take for granted in a world where such things no longer exist. In my reverie, I cruise down to the river in the ERV, strip down to my birthday suit, and plunge in, spraying great, slow motion mouthfuls up and over my head in the dappled sunshine.

EIGHTY-ONE

I am chatting with a cousin I haven't seen in over thirty years when death arrives, her white, crepe-soled shoes quietly kissing the floor. A nurse's aide discretely alerts me to her presence. The few people in the room wordlessly melt away, leaving the three of us alone. Death is more deferential than expected—do I detect a careworn weariness? There's an element of brusque efficiency in her manner that has the effect of heightening my awareness of the room and its contents. Afternoon sunlight honeys the air and ignites the lenses of mother's eyeglasses on the nightstand. A stuffed bear clutching a heart like a shield appears poised to speak. The ambient din of the ward in the empty hours before dinner, subsides to perfect stillness.

Mother lays mummied under layers of sheets, warm blankets, and a heavy quilt. I picture the bedclothes floating majestically skyward, buoyed by the bright bubble of her rising soul, rotating against the ceiling in a pinwheel bloom before everything is abruptly sucked through a small aperture radiating the light of a thousand suns. But death is a quiet, deliberate, and thoughtful operator, left to her own devices, despite our long history of harnessing the harried dowager to our own selfish ends.

I am grateful for one last touch, my whispered apology and farewell delivered, heads touching. Come full circle, we converge intimately, bookending our shared time on earth. Before she lapsed into unconsciousness, Ima Nell talked nonstop as if desperate to disperse the unspent portion of a lavish bequest of words. The gift must have been inordinately generous. She had always been a prodigious talker, on par with an exceptionally gregarious tour guide or stumping candidate, deploying words tactically to win over strangers and establish beachheads of instantaneous intimacy. Words swarmed, overwhelmed, and ultimately prevailed. Their comforting cadence lulled and kept the dreaded vacuum of long, uncomfortable silence at bay.

The day before she takes to her bed for the last time, we sit outdoors on a covered patio, watching afternoon shadows clock around the parking lot, waiting for the rest of the family to arrive. She makes little sense, but keeps alive a furious running commentary. She converses with long dead kin arrayed around her and narrates an ancestral slide show with catty observations and surprisingly hostile asides. There's no hoped for eleventh-hour revelation, no heartfelt words of reconciliation. Apropos of nothing, eyes wide with conviction, she rises suddenly to my father's defense as having been an exemplar of fatherhood, her fury belying uncertainty on the matter. I listen with a perplexed mixture of sadness, irritation, and immersion deep enough to erase the passage of time. Her long, final farewell spins out extravagantly, but ultimately falls thin on the ear.

For the next two days, we cluster around her in vigil. I swap Uranus jokes with my nephew, contemplate proffered morphine syrettes. My brother and his family agonize, delaying an unavoidable departure as long as possible. She lingers, never quite rallying, yet displaying no precipitous signs of decline. I fully expect her to open her eyes, claim to have dozed off for a few minutes and ask for a hairbrush and mirror. People come and go; family not seen in decades, her friends from choir, an overly earnest, telegenic assistant pastor, a rotating clutch of solemn teenaged nurses' aides.

She had fashioned for herself a life as seen through a veil of appearances; doubt and introspection dismissed as little more than shameless self-indulgence, perhaps even dangerous. She kept sorrow at bay and always put past behind. She hungered for attention, sought validation in every exchange. The messy family business of belonging and feeling wanted, of hurt and rejection, the haunting refrain of things left unsaid, were best viewed in the faux-distance of the passenger side mirror.

As a child I had but two essential tasks: divine her moods in order to mollify, please, and deflect, and stand shadowed in awed fealty to my father, an embittered man haunted by ghosts he chose to keep to himself. They bucked strong headwinds from within and without, gales that bedeviled, and left them heedless of life playing out before their eyes. They looked through me, the idealized child alive in their imaginations, certain to appear. Little was expected of me beyond benign compliance, wary vigilance, and willful invisibility. A diminutive Stevens in service to the House of Darlington in Ishiguro's *Remains of the Day*.

The human tragedy unfolding in Flint touches off the dry tinder of longing, shame, and regret left behind in great heaps after her death. That my latent sense of activism is fired at all, is nothing more than an unhappy accident. Had she lived on, my sense of civic responsibility may have remained confined to displaying yard signs. She lived in Michigan nearly fifty years—came of age in the Great Lakes State without once having set foot in The Vehicle City, at least as far as I know.

The temperature of my empathy for Flint's woes had never risen much above simmer. My position on the city's fate, while not one of indifference, was abstracted and intermittent as an AM station at the far end of the dial. *Roger and Me* certainly left a lasting impression, but of Michael Moore himself, rather than his subject. Would Flint's latest round of agonies have galvanized me more than the many insults and deprivations already visited upon the city, had they not become entwined with rage and grief brought about by her long decline and death? Would my anger and sadness have found visceral expression some other way, in some other place?

I inherited her sense of social justice, knee-jerk identification with the oppressed, righteous indignation at the abuse of privilege. She couldn't abide a bully, nor can I. That we reached separate, equally compromised accommodation with my father is, perhaps, our most durable bond. If my ruination were, in fact, inflicted, then she alone was implicated; a failure at the one task with which she had been entrusted. It was an unfortunate myth in whose brackish waters we foundered, only one of us destined to make dry land.

A Good Man. Some say he can't be kept down. Others claim he's hard to find. You'll know him by the way he treats the wait person, holds the door, calls mom on her birthday, puts the seat down, yields to pedestrians, offers his seat to the weary, speaks truth to power, defends the weak. Charlie Brown was proclaimed one on Broadway. I've spent a lifetime alert to him in books, film, song, and on television. Big Bad John, the title character of Jimmy Dean's 1961 hit, a miner who sacrifices himself to save his coal-blackened comrades. Harper Lee's flawed Atticus Finch—the granite visage of the Gregory Peck version. Jeff Daniels's transgressive stage interpretation of Aaron Sorkin's revisionist version. Roy Hobbs, the Bernard Malamud character in *The Natural*. E.B. White's Charlotte A. Cavatica, neither man nor human, but exemplary of the ideal. Sorkin's other flawed male protagonists. Richard Ford's Everyman, Frank Bascombe.

Like Diogenes, I've searched him out—with less cynical intent, I hope. Pete Seeger singing Woody Guthrie. Sitting Bull and his Ghost Dance visions. Dr. Martin Luther King Jr. stepping onto the Edmund Pettus Bridge. Abraham Lincoln stepping off the train at Gettysburg. US Army Warrant Officer Hugh Clowers Thompson Jr. who, in 1968, saved Vietnamese civilians during the My Lai Massacre by training his gunship's weapons on marauding US infantry. Daniel Ellsberg, of

Pentagon Papers fame. Khizer Khan, Gold Star father, proud American Muslim, and keeper of the Constitutional flame. United States Army Lieutenant Colonel Alexander Semyon Vindman, whose quiet, exacting testimony in the Congressional impeachment hearings of Donald J. Trump defined honor and resolute love of country. Senator John Lewis, urging us to get into good trouble. Fred Rogers, humane champion of the dignity of childhood, to name but a few. Surely, I'll be forgiven for including the Honorable Ruth Bader Ginsburg.

The title character in Steven Spielberg's *Saving Private Ryan* survives into old age, returns to the tranquil cemeteries of Normandy, extended family in tow, falls to his knees before Lieutenant John H. Miller's snow-white marker and pleads, "Tell me I've led a good life. Tell me I'm a good man."

A question wrapped in a plea, but it is far from rhetorical. I ask it every day of those closest to me, if not in so many words. I query myself, constantly. The answer Ryan sought wasn't found chiseled on Miller's stone. Neither was it forthcoming from his worried, uncomprehending wife, at least not in the definitive way Ryan longed for. Had the filmmaker deigned Lieutenant Miller survive the war, we can presume he would have spent the rest of his days asking the same question of his wife and high school English Composition students.

My father, like many men, wrestled with this question. He was, tragically, burdened with an answer he found untenable, the only one he could permit himself. This would be our shared legacy. I was a constant reminder of the thing he feared most. If he couldn't bring himself to flee, pronouncing me ruined at least made life a little more bearable.

What would my mother make of my meager attempt to help in Flint? To be judged a good man by one's fellows is a fine thing, but a mother's blessing is pure as water sprung from the cleft of a rock. I like to think she would have been well pleased.

EIGHTY-TWO

t's late July, 2016, and my flirtation with disaster deployment, along with the entire Red Cross relief effort in Flint, is drawing to a close. Not so, the ongoing struggle for clean water. My final water delivery partner speaks in a delicate Dixie drawl. Val was born in St. Louis, but reared in Flint. She has lived here over forty years, yet retains a pleasingly well-worn accent. She's a former nurse who reminds me of my aunt Doris. It could be the cigarettes and dry, rasping laugh. Flirtatious dip of the chin, lazy elongation of the neck, and sidelong cast of the eyes hint at sly seduction. She is among the first class of residents hired by the state to keep Flint's citizens supplied with potable water.

Standpipes, I call them, emergency bypass taps installed to convey that most basic of life's essentials into the kitchens and bathrooms of the city. Nothing fancy, a simple spigot, they get the job done—end of story. I'm training her to deliver water to those most in need. Soon, Val, Flynn, and others will replace Red Cross DRV's, themselves replacements for National Guard troopers and State Police officers, putting me out of the water delivery business for good. I welcome them with open arms. Someone should benefit, in whatever small way, from such a sublime debacle. By lunchtime, Val has confided intimate, harrowing details of her life. A nine-year-old lost to a long battle with cancer, another son debilitated by a head injury inflicted during an assault, a probable hate crime. She hints at dark stretches of despair and other sorrowful things. She calls me darlin'—addresses everyone we meet as sweetie, child, or honey. Hugs for the women, a hand on the arm or back for the men, a big, old Southern smile for all.

"Well, aren't you just the sweetest thing."

"You take care now, this heat's just plain awful, innit?"

"We'll be back next week, hon, don't you worry 'bout it none."

"Wha'cha need darlin'? Lordy, haven't you got the prettiest ole' eyes."

I have nothing to teach her about the job of delivering water in Flint, not one goddamn thing.

The End

ACKNOWLEDGEMENTS

I applaud the people of Flint for their faith and fortitude. I'm honored to have had the opportunity to get to know their fine city a little bit better. I wish to thank those at the American Red Cross East Central Bay-Michigan chapter for the good work they do. I am grateful to Anne Trubek and everyone at Belt Publishing for their support. I especially want to thank my editor, Martha Bayne, for her thoughtful reading and indispensable editorial advice. Thanks also to Dr. Carol Stratman for listening and her extraordinary endurance, and to Thomas Lynch for advice and encouragement in the early going. Finally, eternal thanks to my family and my wife, Sue, my first, foremost, and most important reader.

ABOUT THE AUTHOR

David Hardin is a Michigan poet, writer, and artist. He is the author of two books of poetry, *A Ruinous Thirst* (self-published, 2012) and *Dreaming Bob Wills* (Silverbow Publishing, 2020). His work has also appeared in *3 Quarks Daily*, *Prague Review*, *Drunken Boat*, *Hermes Poetry Journal*, *Dunes Review*, *Epigraph Magazine*, *Loose Change*, *Burningwood Literary Journal*, *ARDOR*, *Carolina Quarterly*, *Madison Review*, the 2014 *Bear River Review*, and elsewhere.

An early excerpt of *Standpipe: Delivering Water in Flint* appeared in the October 23, 2016 online issue of the *Michigan Quarterly Review*.